WORK MATTERS

WORK MATTERS

THE HABIT OF YOUR LIFETIME

Rog Johnson

Copyright 2017 Habits Evangelism, Chicago, IL
All rights reserved.

ISBN: 1545241465
ISBN 13: 9781545241462
Library of Congress Control Number: 2017910358
CreateSpace Independent Publishing Platform
North Charleston, South Carolina

To my dad, Bob Johnson, who worked for forty-seven years seeking little recognition while committing his work to his wife, June, and his sons, Ralph and Roger. Thank you, Dad.

To my wife, Ruth Johnson, who for more than twenty-five years has offered her love and commitment, as well as the steady, productive work that fuels our household. Thank you, Ruth.

CONTENTS

	Preface	ix
	Introduction	xi
Chapter 1	An Anchor for Your Work	1
Chapter 2	What Is Work?	7
Chapter 3	What Work Does: For You, For Others, For God	12
	Real People: Work as Industry Ruby Van Brocklin—candymaker, teacher, farmer	20
	Clinton Stockwell—urban educator, historian, administrator	21
	Today's Worker: Maria's Story	21
Chapter 4	Creation and Production	25
Chapter 5	Energy for Our Work	29
Chapter 6	Is It Fun or Hard Work?	32
	Real People: Working for God Ray Bakke—city pastor and missiologist	38

	Bill Bright—candymaker, campus evangelist, mission executive	38
	Today's Workers: Jane, Jackie, George, Tim	39
Chapter 7	Work: Your Inheritance	45
Chapter 8	Money, Debt, Saving	48
	Real People: Hard Workers	
	Bernie Helgesen—railroader, pilot, capitalist	52
	Wayne Kiser—editor, writer, printer, preacher	52
	Today's Worker: Charley—Off and Running	53
Chapter 9	Get Moving: Making Work a Habit	56
Chapter 10	Accept Work	62
Chapter 11	Prepare for Work	67
	Real People: Committed Workers	
	Herman Mueller—metallurgist and blacksmith	72
	Jim Garrett—real-estate broker, baseball umpire	72
	Today's Workers: Betsy and Bill Hopkins, Work for Life	73
Chapter 12	Succeed and Prosper	77
Chapter 13	Mentor Others	81
Chapter 14	Why We Need More Workers	84

PREFACE

Work Matters: The Habit of Your Lifetime is written largely for instruction, correction, and reproof. But it is also written to inspire readers to experience the joy and satisfaction found in productive work. Read the text for the lessons stated and explained in each chapter, but also read this book for the human stories laced throughout the text and concentrated in four special sections: between chapters 3 and 4, 6 and 7, 8 and 9, and 11 and 12. Each of these story sections begins with two real-life stories of excellent workers—people I have known personally who have left a mark upon my own notion of what quality work is all about. These mini-bios move quickly. Gain all you can from the few sentences I have written.

Following each "Real People" section is a selection of "Today's Workers"—true-to-life fiction illustrating several of the work or production principles I have stated. Any resemblance to real personal vignettes is entirely coincidental. These are fictional stories written to illustrate important points of the text. Please enjoy them as such.

In fact, enjoy the entire book! And address any comments my way at rogerjohnson3115@gmail.com.

Remember, our work matters.

INTRODUCTION

WORK IS PARAMOUNT. It pays our way in life. It gives us a reason to get up each day. It describes in large measure who we are and how we are wired as human beings. Work provides each person with both a public image and a good measure of personal meaning for life.

Work used to take first place in both personal and professional conversations. As we move deeper into this twenty-first century, friendly conversations focus more on how we feel, our political and social opinions, or even what's trending on our playlists. A 2016 *Chicago Tribune* survey showed that 50 percent of the city's eighteen- to thirty-two-year-old men spend thirty to thirty-five hours per week playing video games. We have traded work for entertainment; we have swapped production for a bit of digital excitement.

As you read *Work Matters*, you will hear a challenge to use your abilities and energies to produce at full capacity. You will understand why people work and what is special about your call to work. Hopefully, you will delight in your life possibilities when you seek meaning in your work and begin to love that tired sense of accomplishment.

Like others, you may ask, "Why produce to full capacity?" or "Why work at all?" Simply put, we work to earn a material living—it takes money to live. Another answer involves what our work results in. Our economy needs what we produce, and we need to see much of our production become useful to the economy.

But another part of our human identity is also involved. We have the need to occupy ourselves with the bus we drive, the people we manage, the boss we serve, the computer we tap away at, and the meals we prepare. We need to throw ourselves into the difficult, joyous, meaningful, and meaningless tasks that occupy and engage our persons.

Often, work tells us a lot about ourselves—even defines us. At the very least, work needs to occupy us. It does not always have to satisfy and replenish us. Occupying us may be good enough, at least for a time.

The following chapters focus particularly on the nature of work and the habits we will need to start and complete our work. I will also focus on choosing work and then making the needed adjustments when paying work disappears—something that will happen to most of us. I will also focus on the prerequisites for work: anchors, disciplines, direction, and will.

While work may not be the most important part of your life, it is near the top. You will spend over forty years working. Make these years good and productive. Also make them meaningful. Even as you produce valuable things, let the work that occupies you produce value within you.

Rog Johnson – Chicago, Illinois – 2017

CHAPTER 1

AN ANCHOR FOR YOUR WORK

ANYONE CAN WORK; anyone can produce things and get paid for his or her work. But to do meaningful work, one has to have an anchor—a person to whom one is bound and position to which one is tethered. Then our work efforts acquire a reason and purpose.

The notion of an anchor made sense a hundred years ago. Weights and fasteners that pinned down floating objects were invaluable. Ships needed heavy and obvious anchors to remain in safe harbors. Homes and barns needed deep, heavy foundations anchoring them to the earth. Any human-built object needed screws, nails, or fasteners to hold it together in the face of destructive forces.

We humans still need to be anchored. We're naturally mobile and wandering. Our curiosity and creativity (and yes, our laziness!) drives us away from our primary relationships and allegiances. In order for our work to remain focused and meaningful, we need the power of an anchor that will always hold us.

Jesus is the anchor (personified) who provides us with the meaning we need for our life work. He is God Almighty in his identity, and he is the lover of humans in his function. He can redeem and care for our souls. Jesus gave his life for us, and then from his death, he resurrected himself to new life. He accomplished our salvation, and he went on to build an eternal home for all his followers.

We should first ask, "Why an anchor at all?" Does a modern, agile, and adaptive life need to be held fast when we now have so many good options to choose from?

Our array of choices seems like a great add-on, even a blessing, at first glance. But some reflection offers us a wise perspective. Multiple media feeds keep us busy considering various, even conflicting, ideas. While we enjoy that range of thought, we easily become confused by the sheer abundance of smart-sounding ideas. One is quick, another is clever, and yet another seems to have the wisdom we crave. But why choose any single path when you've already traveled far enough to forget your starting place on this grand adventure?

> *We should first ask, "Why an anchor at all?" Does a modern, agile, and adaptive life need to be held fast when we now have so many good options to choose from?*

It's time to reach back and discover your places of origin: family, friends, towns, schools, values, and dreams—they all go into making you the person you are right now.

I was born in 1951 in suburban Chicago—River Grove, to be exact. Mom and Dad were blue-collar workers, usually working three jobs between the two of them. They were thrifty, Bible-believing Fundamentalists who were skeptical of too much education. Their idea of good music ranged somewhere between Lawrence Welk and George Beverly Shea. Bob and June Johnson ran very little risk of shocking friends and relatives with expensive vacations or highbrow culture. We shopped at Sears, seldom ate out, and never went to movies. Life was simple and clear cut.

But answering the question "Where did I come from?" requires deeper history than the baby boom or even Mom and Dad's Depression-era values. Because Fundamentalist Christian faith was so important for both Bob and June Johnson, I'll need to take you back to the roots of Fundamentalism—several years before Mom and Dad were born in 1920.

Their own Scandinavian families came to Chicago around 1910 and quickly put themselves on a suburban success track. Thrift was inbred, along with patriotism, family loyalty, a great desire for God, and an equally great desire to work for a living as well as a personal identity.

To understand my roots, I pay attention to the lessons of the Fundamentalist-Modernist Controversy of the early twentieth century, the antecedents of which go back to America's Bible-and-evangelism culture of the 1870s and 1880s. Without D. L. Moody's salvation sermons of the 1860s, I doubt that I would ever be the latter-day Fundamentalist that I am today. The Bible, evangelism, and Fundamentalist faith are all anchors for my present-day life, work, and faith. Each of us needs to look back to find the anchors that hold our present life and propel our future mission.

Something more about a good anchor: it stays put and in so doing provides a great amount of meaning with a minimum amount of effort. A fishing boat's anchor may be dropped just once, allowing the angler to explore a wide pool of water. A screw properly set doesn't have to be replaced or removed. Likewise, life anchors don't move and often grow stronger as they remain in place. Each remembrance only adds meaning to the anchor's place in our lives.

Before raising your antenna to my worn-out metaphors, consider the power of both the person Jesus and the image of God's Son as the anchor we each need in our lives.

Jesus fits the need for a personal anchor by transcending our lives and personal needs. As God's Son, he is God himself who came to live a human life, die for our sins, and redeem us all for eternal life with him. He has the scope (eternal, powerful, presence) that we want in a life anchor.

But then, Jesus is also effective in accomplishing an anchor's most important task—remaining in place and holding on to the tether. Jesus remains where he was originally set: "Jesus Christ is the same yesterday and today and forever" (Heb. 13:8). While Jesus remains the same and in the same place, his strong connection to us extends far enough that he allows us to discover many of the great joys of life as well as many of the dangers that he continually keeps us from falling into. Jesus is always present with us and keeps us connected to our origins. Jesus—more than just a saving lifeline—is a loving protector and connector. He will not let us go.

But then think with me of the ways in which Jesus the anchor actually locates, stabilizes, and nurtures our growth and development. By his omniscience, Jesus knows where we are and who we are long before we can even ask those questions. He is the source of all meaning and identity; hence he knows the answers to our questions of selfhood and life direction.

Jesus stabilizes us as we explore our life's territory. While being the anchor, he is also the life preserver. Jesus keeps us afloat and free from ultimate harm as we check out the varieties of life in the waters around us. Some creatures are sharks: dangerous and deadly. We're protected. Some fish are edible and life giving. Jesus offers all these species within easy reach, all within the abundant and life-giving water in which we exist. Without such a life element, we would move nowhere nor could we even exist.

Let's return to our work. It may be a chosen profession or a temporary task. Hopefully it pays, but it may be a family or volunteer role. Whatever the nature of our work, Jesus provides us the set of origins we need as a reference point whenever the tasks we take on become confusing or contradictory.

Think of your own career vision and goals that you adopted as a young person—perhaps during your twenties or maybe a bit later in life. You knew your life's work was just what you had been preparing yourself for. The people, the corporation, the job description, and your own personal gifts were all coming together like a bright constellation in the night sky. Everything looked and felt right until your dream boss left for a better assignment or until the customer base inexplicably dried up or until you found your best coworker was actually your competitor—ready to seize your job out from under you. At any of those times, your dream became a nightmare. You needed an anchor, or you simply needed a better option than the job that used to fit you so perfectly.

Anchors are a big help when we make our way through rough waters. Your boat may be about to capsize, but with a solid anchor, you can always pull yourself close to your original mooring.

At other times we face the opposite danger—a problem we neither see nor feel. It's the danger of pleasant, calm seas that still cause you to drift too far offshore for your own good. Imagine the dream job you thought about a moment ago. Maybe you succeeded in it beyond your wildest dreams. You earned raises and respect. New tasks made your days fulfilling. You helped your company profit and fulfill its mission. And it all came to you so easily.

Until a friend (or competitor) saw that you no longer cared deeply for your coworkers, let alone new clients. You began taking things for granted rather than learning new lessons to teach others. "What happened?" your friend asked, and you had to face the fact that work had been going *too smoothly*. You had strayed so far from your anchor that you hadn't realized how lost you were. Things all around you looked good, but where was your anchor? Where was your lifeline?

Your anchor can be steady, strong, and unmovable, but if you can no longer find your tether line, you are in deep trouble. As we keep our eyes on Jesus, our anchor, we find the way back to not just our origins but our first love!

Remember your creator and how he loved you deeply: fitting, molding, and hardening you into the person he created you to be. The creator is a lover, a wise parent, and a skillful coach. The creator, Jesus, is a good God and a great anchor for you.

As we keep our eyes on Jesus, our anchor, we find the way back to not just our origins but our first love!

Maybe you already know Jesus as your anchor and enjoy that experience. Perhaps you know who you can reach out to when the pressures at work get beyond you. Perhaps you've gone right to the anchor when you can't go to anyone in confidence at your workplace. You know the meaning of having an anchor for your work—all the hours you invest in carving out a life and making a living.

If you don't have Jesus as your anchor when starting a new job, you will need him there to hold you steady very soon. Count on it, and prepare yourself ahead of time.

In beginning a new job, we often buy specific clothes we will need or the right laptop and smartphone. We would be making a mistake beginning the job without the proper equipment to accomplish all we can. Before taking another step, reach back and find your anchor. Locate Jesus, and position yourself close to him and his words for your life. Make sure you have a good sight line for finding him—whether you're socked in by fog, bounced around in a storm, or enjoying calm waters ahead. You'll need to keep your eye on Jesus if you're to have a chance to take up your life's mission. Why an anchor for your work? Because the anchor will be there whether you see it or not! Yes, your anchor is right around you, always ready to help you find your best way. Find that best anchor of all. Hold close; keep Jesus in sight and in mind. Make sure your tether line is close at hand.

CHAPTER 2

WHAT IS WORK?

We want to answer that simple question in complex, nuanced ways. We want to include many types of work and many people from a variety of talents, temperaments, and backgrounds. But in the end, a simple definition of work suffices for most of us.

Work is our personal investment of time and energy intended to produce a defined, desired result. Let's add just a few more things about work:

- Work is God's command and calling: "The Lord God took the man and put him in the Garden of Eden to work it and keep it" (Gen. 2:15).
- Work presumes itself upon us whether we like it or not.
- It's great when work satisfies our passions, but satisfaction is not part of the work equation.
- Work benefits us (financially, spiritually, and physically) or at least it ought to!

- Work is something we do in preparation for something else (i.e., we work to buy a home; we work to graduate from college), but it is also something that we do for our entire life—and then on into our eternal life! "His servants shall serve him" (Rev. 22:3).
- Work is usually best defined by tasks, hours, and pay. Humans need limits, benchmarks, and goals in order to measure what we are doing with our lives.
- Work—real work—is exhausting. It tires us out and sometimes satisfies us immensely. It will always be one of life's perplexing conundrums.

Eric Leaf, my father's uncle, was born in Sweden in 1888. He came to America in 1908 and farmed for the rest of his life in Macedonia, Iowa. When I first met Eric in 1959, he was essentially retired but still looked every bit the farmer: bib overalls, a basket of eggs from the henhouse, farm reports from Omaha, few words, large hands, and a will to be out in the wheat fields with a dozen strong farmhands each July. Eric's work and identity were linked through his fifty-plus years as a farmer. He had been a hired hand, husband to the farm owner's daughter, and then an independent grower. His identity as a good farmer outlived him by decades.

Barbara Weith grew up two houses from me in suburban River Grove, Illinois. We Johnsons were the Fundamentalists on the block; the Weiths were solid Lutherans (German, choral singers, beer drinkers, and Concordia College graduates). We knew who we were, and they knew even better who they were. We were not exactly friends, but we respected each other. Concordia's BA in Education led Barbara right to her work as a Lutheran school teacher and pastoral assistant at St. Luke's Church in Chicago. Barbara died in her early fifties, and probably would have never retired if given that option. The Lutheran

Church was her life and work—sometimes forty-five hours a week, sometimes sixty or seventy. Barbara was always ready to do what was asked of her.

Bob Johnson, my dad, grew up on Chicago's northwest side. The son of Swedish immigrants, Dad's great claim to fame was his work record: Clark & Barlow Hardware prior to World War II, Tuttle & Kift Electric throughout the 1950s, followed by twenty-seven years at Sears Roebuck. Dad was sick only a couple of days through his forty-five working years. Talking shop, whether hardware or catalog sales, trumped all other topics. Dad lived through the Great Depression—a tougher experience than any World War II adventures. Once through with the Army, he vowed to earn and save his way out of any future depression, even if that meant sixty-hour workweeks.

Work consumes many lives. It easily becomes too much, overwhelming the desires to love people and love God, to celebrate one's family and celebrate the riches of the earth. Work takes on a devouring life of its own—begetting more work, more hours, and less room for anything else enriching to one's soul.

To be fair, work is actually an extension of the human soul—even when work hours are tedious, painful, and nonproductive. Work reaches into our beings and draws out some of the best of our hidden selves. I am deeply made up of each occupation that I have pursued: editor, warehouseman, umpire, pastor, salesman, evangelist, and gardener. Each is in some way my passion. I cannot leave one behind.

> **Work consumes many lives. It easily becomes too much, overwhelming the desires to love people and love God, to celebrate one's family and celebrate the riches of the earth.**

Once begun, work keeps going. In a world that questions the beginning of adult life, work is a defining trait of real adults. We may not love or even like our work, but we work because it pays and is ultimately redeeming. We are hesitant to leave our work, whether at age sixty-two, sixty-six, or beyond. Work pays—just begin counting the ways.

Work is a big chunk of our lives (perhaps twenty to sixty hours per week). It is a commitment that dominates our waking hours. We need to be sold on our work and the value it adds to our life and many lives around us. Currently, I work twenty-five hours each week as a gardener—and it exhausts me! That means that I'm throwing myself into something I like doing (tending and selling flowers, trees, and shrubs). I like investing myself in leaves, roots, and soil each day. I'm satisfied, if not always enriched, by my work. Work should give each of us the satisfaction of investing our energies into something that we deem worthwhile.

I have already hinted at the notion that work is God's calling for each of us. The Genesis account tells us that God's intention has always been for humans to work—first in tending the garden world he created for us. We were to use the grains and fruits to feed ourselves and then invest great parts of the harvest and its seeds for the future. After sin entered the world, work got much harder (Gen. 3:17–19). Humans were called to save in big ways, plan ahead for future generations, and cultivate not only the soil but their own hearts and minds with a work ethic. We are born to be God's workers in the world he has created—and then re-created to desire and enjoy God's presence with us. This news is exciting, and it means that our work will go on long after we die and pass from this world's existence. We are born again, unto Jesus Christ's salvation and unto work in God's "new heaven and new earth" (Rev. 21). We practice at our work now for the perfected work that will one day be our calling.

Yes, work is hard in this sin-filled world. It takes more energy and effort to design a great digital device than it should. It takes more patience and sleepless nights to raise three children than it should. It takes more love and wisdom to heal a marriage bent on divorce than it should. Work means a lot of hard and aching times, tired heads, weary muscles, confused motives, and frayed nerve endings. Many times we just aren't ready for all that our work takes out of us.

But work is still God's will and calling for our lives. Leisure is needed to rest our bodies and souls, to recover and begin work again. But when leisure dominates our lives, meaning vacates our existence, love dissipates, and eternal purpose gives way to fleeting amusement. Leisure is necessary, but it's no way to live.

Seek meaningful work; seek any kind of productive work at all. Focus on what you are good at, what you are gifted and talented at doing. But don't get too hung up about working outside your calling. The hardest and ugliest work still needs to be done! The most difficult people need to team up with others by working together. Few of us are so talented as to accomplish our chosen task all by ourselves.

If you're already working, keep working and celebrate your efforts. If you are not working, begin quickly! Then maximize and leverage your skills, your productivity, and your pay.

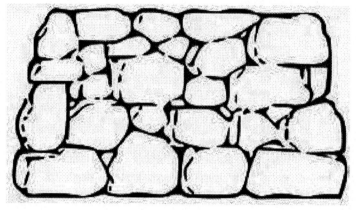

CHAPTER 3

WHAT WORK DOES: FOR YOU, FOR OTHERS, FOR GOD

WORK PROVIDES YOU with direction. Yes, a job points you in the direction where you need to invest your time, energy, and skills. Life is pretty much like an Individual Retirement Account (IRA). Short-term results barely show up, and the IRA kind of stays where it is at. But as you invest for decades, you see healthy growth. During good times, you are quite amazed at how your money grows. Exponential growth is amazing.

While most of us change jobs too often, we continue doing the kind of work that we are good at. Wherever I've worked, I have always been a researcher and organizer of information. Sometimes I come up with good results. Other times I just sort facts and offer new ways to look at them. But I gain a lot of direction through my research. Inventory tables tell me why we produce metals, ice cream, and Bibles. Personal interviews give me a grid to understand people around me. Even ball-and-strike counts while umpiring home plate for lackluster baseball teams provide the direction to get through a smothering ball game. If we don't have direction, life runs us over. Even when we have direction, life still remains very tough to deal with.

The very act of going to work requires direction, discipline, and effort—effort to get up two hours before the workday begins, discipline to follow a pregame set of habits that makes the workday possible, and direction to stay on a course that gets you through the day. Focus and direction are critical to accomplishing anything.

Think of direction in another way.

On a busy downtown corner, some people have no idea whether they are headed north, south, east, or west. They look for landmarks, faces, or something in the buildings that line the street. When everything looks familiar, we often lose our way.

Often these days, we lose our vocational direction, our spiritual direction, or our relational direction—even our direction for health and well-being. That is a serious case of getting lost.

Think back to times in your life when you knew exactly what you were doing. You knew why prior jobs were important and what type of job you would do next. These are the sweet spots in our careers. If you have known them, you are fortunate.

Ingrain this exercise in your memory: (1) know exactly what you are doing, (2) know why you are doing it, and (3) know how your work is preparing you for the job you will be doing next. That is what directional work is all about.

The 2016 Chicago Cubs prepared, worked, and cruised their way to a World Series Championship. They basically won two of every three games, combining timely hitting with overpowering pitching and defense. All twenty-five teammates played their hearts out for each other. The Cubs knew their direction for 2016 and beyond. As a result, they should win in the years ahead.

Knowing your direction and role at work is huge. It is related to identity, yet it is more connected to movement. Direction determines where me move and if we move at all. Direction is much like an arrow—always pointing to a defined location.

Work also provides rewards—money to spend and resources to save for the future. If you are working hard but not getting enough in the way of rewards, do something about it! Otherwise, you are probably volunteering. That is fine, but it is not the kind of work we are talking about.

Pay is determined by what you do, how hard you work, the amount of time you work, and most of all the market for your work. As you decide on your expectations for your work, consider the market around you. There is probably little market for secondary math teachers in a Del Webb retirement community. But there will be a large market for physical therapists in that very same place. Consider the important factors, and then throw yourself into your work. You will be amazed at the rewards that come your way.

Do not hesitate to set healthy growth goals for your salary. If your pay is not growing, your skill set is probably not growing as well. Set your financial goals reasonably high, and talk to both peers and supervisors about those goals to make them realistic.

Work provides us with lots of meaning. We spend numerous hours and significant moments of our lives at work. These investments ought to result in a coherent meaning for life, or we will find ourselves suffering from career bankruptcy after only a few years.

Increasing numbers of people are preparing themselves for significant work and landing jobs that provide good salaries and benefits. But somewhere along the way, workers are hitting the wall, realizing that their paychecks and stock options are not worth enough in comparison to continuing education options. The employee finds himself wanting something different and wanting something more. How does the high-performing worker continue to find meaning in his work?

Work provides us with lots of meaning. We spend numerous hours and significant moments of our lives at work. These investments ought to result in a coherent meaning for life, or we will find ourselves suffering from career bankruptcy after only a few years.

Take some time to reflect on the point of your work. Many people work at routine, repetitive jobs for many years. They find satisfaction and meaning in the people whom they have helped through all the tasks they do. Other people weave themselves into their company's identity and in so doing find special meaning for their lives. But a better way to find meaning is to examine what attracted you to your employment in the first place. If you work in health care, chances are your values are centered on healthy bodies and minds. If you build new corporations, you are probably proud of many kinds of growing companies. If you make electrical switches, you are probably delighted by the quality and quantity of products that you have churned out year after year. Production is good, and increased production is usually better. Great meaning can be derived from profit, increased production, and expansion. If growth is what you value, then take great pride in all the growth that you make happen.

A certain level of meaning is crucial to our ongoing existence. In his classic *Man's Search for Meaning*, Viktor Frankl drives home the message that "he who has a *why* to live for, can bear almost any *how*." Meaning is found in the questions (and answers) as to why we love those who seem unlovely, why we remain loyal to our family even when our family cannot find a way to be loyal to us. Similarly, our search for meaning in work is often tied to the small deposits of meaning that we put into our daily lives—our work habits. Managing a corporation's Accounts Payable becomes meaningful when we help build our company's habits around investing in significant people and their causes. Library databases may become significant if we make new, meaningful acquisitions an important part of our work. Garden care becomes meaningful if we first make sure to spend time with plants (and customers) needing the most attention.

We may not be saviors of lost causes, but we can be important voices speaking of people who are not important to others. We can promote those left behind, reverse unjust priorities, or simply help the C student move up to a B. It is worth the effort. And anything worth the effort results in greater meaning than we previously thought possible.

Your work should do lots for you. But what about your work and your customers, your friends, your family, your coworkers, and even observers of your work? How does your work impact all these people?

By its nature, your work is not private. Most often, you work with people in teams. And your income probably supports several people other than yourself. The time you spend working has a big impact upon your spouse, family, friends, and even coworkers. Even where you work, how you work and what you do can have a huge impact on people all around you. Work today often feels like a relationship between you and your boss, but in reality your work creates a web of important relationships.

Your boss and other supervisors: As you complete your tasks proficiently, your boss is pleased and looks good to his colleagues, including the company's leadership. He increasingly relies on you as his go-to worker who sets the standard for all other workers. A sound working relationship is built, and standards for production and service are set that reverberate throughout the company's culture. Good work really does matter.

Coworkers: They usually rely upon you as a skilled worker. Everyone needs help in the workplace, and if you are the person who others can go to for advice, skills, and the habits to perform a job well, you are exactly the coworker they need. You will be trusted and respected, treated well by everyone, and probably advance in the company's structures. Coworkers count.

Your spouse and immediate family members: Your spouse counts on you to hold up your end of the economic bargain with a steady, dependable paycheck. The money you bring home helps in paying the big items: housing, transportation, food, and clothing. How much you make may not be as important as the consistent work you do, providing your household with the economic power for spending and saving. If you have a good savings plan, you will bring added value to your household package.

Your work also makes connections to the outside world for your spouse and family. You allow your family to relate to a defined community and a way of producing wealth. For most of my career, I have worked in the Christian, nonprofit sector. The majority of relationships my wife and I still enjoy are with pastors, writers, community developers, missionaries, and fundraisers. While religious work does not pay big, my work relationships throughout the years have proven to be a rich network.

We like to think that our friends know and love us for who we are, not what we do. Truth be told, what we do marks us as worthwhile people. We like our friends to be people whom we can count on. Employed workers are just that—people who have proven that they can be counted on: to show up, to produce, to earn, save and help others in need. Workers are people of character as well as people of some resource. That makes them valuable as friends, helpers, and advisors.

Our work impacts people around us by the expertise we develop on the job. One of the first things my current boss told a group of us as new hires was that we needed to view ourselves as "experts in our designated areas of home care and design." Each new employee came into that meeting as a salesperson. Yet more than half of the customers who come to my garden center want and need an expert's advice before they are confident to buy something. If you work in one job for more than a few months at a time, you need to develop an expertise in your assigned area. Be an expert, simply because others around you are viewing you as an expert, whether you asked for that role or not!

I assume the reality of God as the agent of creation and redemption for those of us fortunate to be part of his world. In the opening chapter of Genesis, God creates all things in his proper order and sits back after each day of creation—pleased with his creation. On the sixth day in which God creates human beings, he is especially delighted with his creation, for he has now breathed into these humans his own creative inspiration to steward, tend, and grow the godly creation. He now has people in place who can preserve the creation and make something out of it. Indeed, God has given men and women the role of workers in his garden. We are creative and productive people who have the responsibility for nature's health and production.

Then in the second chapter of Genesis, a defining sin nature enters the human equation. We will never escape the fact that our work upon this earth became a lot harder. Crops suffered from disease, food became difficult to produce, and metals were tough to extract from the ground. While production was still possible, it became a lot harder than God had first intended. Work became a tough reality; scarcity, rot, decay, loss, and theft are now realities.

Indeed, God has given men and women the role of workers in his garden. We are creative and productive people who have the responsibility for nature's health and production.

Has God saddled us with this difficult version of work as a curse? Some might say yes, but that is hardly a fulfilling version of the truth. Rather, work is truly a gift and blessing that humans are now to throw themselves into in order to live, thrive, profit, and understand their God-given roles. In a big way, work is our way of understanding who we are and who God is. In understanding God as Lord of all material and production, we begin to understand what obeying and following God is all about. The person who seeks only pleasure is not following or obeying God. His allegiance is to himself and like-minded pleasure-loving humans. But when we subject ourselves to God, we put our own pleasures in a secondary role, seeking first to enjoy God's pleasure. As work drives us to God's desire for his creation, we begin to become Jesus's disciples with a re-created identity as workers in the divine creation.

Work binds us to God in a humbling way. We humans can only create a small (though important) part of all that needs to be built, repaired, and tended. We quickly realize that our significance as God's workers is measured not in vast quantity but in meaningful chunks of quality work. As we instruct and raise up one more skilled worker, we are doing God's work. As we pioneer one more set of good software, we are doing God's own work. As we sell another line of quality products, we are again doing God's work in stewarding, producing, and caring for all creation.

God is impacted by our work as well. In all likelihood, he is delighted by what we do—if in good quality and good spirit.

Most importantly, we engage ourselves in the tasks God has given us to accomplish at a particular time. Beware of making too much of calling. Finding meaning in our work at a particular moment is quite enough to fulfill ourselves, benefit those close to us, and to praise God as the instruments of his hands.

REAL PEOPLE: WORK AS INDUSTRY
RUBY VAN BROCKLIN–CANDY MAKER, TEACHER, FARMER

Ruby Rowland was born in rural Winnebago County, Illinois, with farming in her blood. Though she loved the land and rich friendships of Illinois's prairies, she moved to Chicago prior to World War II to study at Moody Bible Institute and work at Mars Candy Company: Snickers, Milky Ways, chocolates! Ruby made time for worship, service, and great friendships at the tiny River Grove Bible Chapel in a nearby suburb. She worked hard, led an active social life, and traveled widely. But work at Mars Candy dominated her life in the 1950s. To Ruby's delight, many of her best friends worked right with her at the candy factory.

At nearly forty, Ruby renewed her friendship with a Winnebago County classmate whose wife had recently died. Leo Van Brocklin and Ruby kept up a city-country courtship until they were married in 1959 at the Bible Church in River Grove. Ruby started all over on the farm in Leaf River, Illinois. Once again she fed chickens, tended a garden, and brought in harvests. In 1960 she took on a new role as a mom to her daughter Lorna. Each day was more than full-time work, and Ruby loved it. She tackled every job that came her way—cooking, teaching, driving, and planting—and lived on the Leaf River farm until her passing at age ninety-nine. Hard work produces corn, dairy products, and longevity as well.

CLINTON STOCKWELL—URBAN EDUCATOR, HISTORIAN, ADMINISTRATOR

Clinton Stockwell has come a long way from his roots in Baton Rouge, Louisiana. Raised Southern Baptist, he attended Baptist college and seminary in New Orleans. Clinton maximized his natural bent for research in pursuit of several degrees at universities in Chicago and Toronto. Beginning in the 1970s, he served the academy and the church as a scholar (noted for urban bibliographies), professor, writer, and administrator. Clinton invested the lion's share of his energies as director and professor at Chicago Semester—an urban internship program he reinvented to mentor Midwest college students for urban careers.

Clinton worked in both research and academic administration. He built a vast body of annotated literature in the fields of public policy, urban theology, and city histories. And he has now embarked on a new phase of ground-breaking research with a major work on US general and president Ulysses Grant.

Regarding his work disciplines, Clinton Stockwell speaks in wise ways, "How I work as a teacher is one thing, how I worked as a director another, and how I function on church committees yet another style. Focus, self-discipline, and sense of mission are all very important. So are time management, interpersonal support, and encouragement." Now retired from Chicago Semester, Clinton continues to teach at National Louis University and the University of Chicago's Graham Center while pursuing writing projects in both Chicago and Galena, Illinois.

TODAY'S WORKER: MARIA'S STORY

Like some 14 million single parents in America, Maria has the daunting task of raising her four- and six-year-old boys. At age thirty-four, three years past her divorce, Maria works thirty-five hours per week at her phone-sales job, earning about $31,000 per year, in addition to the $750 per month she receives in child support. After scraping together $1,300 in condo payments each month, after-school and daycare, groceries, a bit of recreation and all the rest, she saves just enough for a twice-a-year trip back to her mother's big house in Cleveland.

What does Maria really need? By her own admission, she needs a good husband and the accompanying transformation in life, income, and parenting capabilities. Whether she finds that husband or not, Maria needs a second-income stream that makes sense for her present lifestyle in Jacksonville, Florida. She likes her job and her few helpful friends at the office. They provide part of the joy she is seeking, right along with her adorable (if still challenging) little boys. She would like to keep her sales job at its present level but find a way to add a much-needed $15K–$20K to her annual income.

Recently one of her coworkers, Gloria, completed real-estate classes and is on her way to being licensed to sell in Florida. Gloria is excited about her move and is encouraging Maria to take the same training course and move toward her own license as well. Maria has always been good at cold calls and enjoys meeting people's needs. She likes homes, apartments, and condos; and she knows that if she has the proper time available, she could succeed in part-time real estate.

Maria needs a second-income stream that makes sense for her present lifestyle.

But Maria is stressed with raising her two boys and scared that she might be taking on too much. More than anything, she does not want to make a major mistake that will set her life back by several years.

Her fear is telling her that $30K–$40K a year plus child support will be okay to support her lifestyle while the boys make it through the elementary grades. But she also knows that she has no chance of owning her own home and saving for any sort of higher education for the boys. She will be safe, but she will be short-changing both the boys and her own future. It is not a pretty picture; it is just safe for right now.

Still, her big dreams are telling her that she can put in forty-five to fifty-five hour weeks at two jobs and perhaps even double her income over the next five years. It will not be easy, but Maria has always had an ambitious streak frustrated by an incomplete college degree, a bad marriage, and fear! She knows that right now is the time to become a great mom and great provider.

Maria began listening more closely to what her friend Gloria told her about real estate. The classes were fun and productive, and Gloria is already earning $1,200 a month in commissions as she begins her second career. Maria got interested enough to ask Gloria to help her find childcare to cover the Monday–Wednesday 6:00–8:00 p.m. real-estate classes. She has now decided to jump in, work hard, and do it!

After completing the September–December classes, Maria found a part-time position with the same realty firm where Gloria worked. Maria started out fast in the winter-spring home-buying season. She learned lots about the business and about her own gifts for understanding people, selling, and buying. Like Gloria, Maria soon saw an additional $900–$1,200 per month in her bank account.

Let's move ahead to the following September. Maria could hardly believe the transformation that had taken place. Raising her two boys was more difficult than ever. Danny was now in kindergarten while Lance is a second grader. They did not understand what Mom was doing, away from the condo so much, but they liked the fact that she was a happy person. They also liked it when she spent Saturday and Sunday evenings totally interested in what was going on with them.

Maria has now completed eighteen house transactions and has started to gain the confidence that veteran Realtors talked about in classes ten months back. Her additional income from North Florida Properties has enabled her and the boys to plan a special fall weekend getaway—to Sea World no less. She's been able to start a house account as well as a boys' college fund. It is all an uphill battle, and she is tired most weeks. But she is also excited about being a mom, a sales agent, and a Realtor.

In thinking through how her life has changed, Maria has little time for reflection or questions. But she is looking forward to her date next Friday night with Chris—another part-time home seller who started at North Florida Properties just two months after Maria began her second career. Chris is working hard at two jobs, just like Maria and Gloria. And he is excited enough to think of further commercial training and going full time in the booming Florida coast real-estate market. Friday night will be filled with good food, a great movie, and lots of dreams.

A year back, Maria made one of the most important decisions of her career. She knows that her decision was right and well timed. She also knows that her commitment to work long, hard hours was the best of all. Great work makes for a great life.

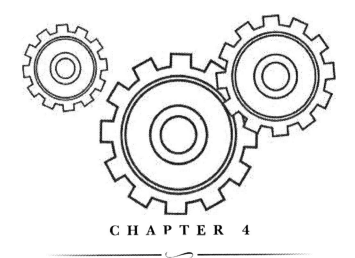

CHAPTER 4

CREATION AND PRODUCTION

WORK CHANNELS OUR energies into the splendid arenas of creation and production. While creation is ultimately God's work, people are gifted with a great measure of creative genius—imitating God's something-from-nothing production.

Reflect on your own best work. Perhaps you are thinking of a splendid career moment when you accomplished things you had never before tried. You jump-started your career and were congratulated by leaders and coworkers alike. You instantly knew that your own discipline would never be the same. You had set a new standard.

Creating is the act of stepping outside your comfort zone and making something happen—bigger and more valuable than you thought possible. Sometimes it happens suddenly. Other times the creative process is just that—a long journey in building a new product or a series of small steps leading to an important result. Creating and producing are the critical results of your work. They validate the time and effort you invest.

Truth be told, production is every bit as important a part of our work as is origin, discipline, and salary. Your work must result in something that can be named—even if what you produce is not as tangible a product as the latest Android phone. If you are a teacher, your work may result in students' new understanding of themselves. If you are a grocery-store cashier, your work may result in satisfied customers and increased profit margins. If you are a website developer, your work may result in the ease, speed, and beauty that an Internet user enjoys. There should always be a named result of our work that we can point to with pride.

Creating is the act of stepping outside your comfort zone and making something happen—bigger and more valuable than you thought possible. Sometimes it happens suddenly. Other times the creative process is just that—a long journey in building a new product or a series of small steps leading to an important result.

As we enjoy that product, we are providing our work with reason and meaning. If we can point to a good reason for what we do, we experience meaning that is critical to our continued work. We desire compliments, but often we are faced with blank stares as we present our best efforts. In the face of decidedly mixed responses, it is important that we continue to produce good quantities of our best products and build into those products our own creative genius.

We humans are created to invent, build, and produce. We each have distinct souls, and we each have talents for producing products by which we are known. Each of us can be a great and memorable worker. Achievement is a matter of exerting the effort to exceed our existing standards.

At its best, real production is more than dreaming, thinking, or talking—important as those stages might be. Production is a matter of will and translating energy into action. Good major-league hitters are conscious of thinking too much. They know that they have only .4 seconds from recognizing the spin and location of a ninety-eight-miles-per-hour fastball until the pitch is past them. Base hits come by quick muscle response (analysis is left for postgame video sessions). Productive people have a will to respond. Essential to production is a quick, first-strike capability—the active genius that Johann Wolfgang von Goethe once identified:

> "Concerning all acts of initiative and creation, there is one elementary truth that ignorance of which kills countless ideas and splendid plans: that the moment one definitely commits oneself, then Providence moves too. All sorts of things occur to help one that would never otherwise have occurred. A whole stream of events issues from the decision, raising in one's favor all manner of unforeseen incidents and meetings and material assistance, which no man could have dreamed would have come his way. Whatever you can do, or dream you can do, begin it. Boldness has genius, power, and magic in it. Begin it now." (Goethe's *Faust*, lines 214–30, translated by John Anster, 1835)

Producing a valuable product flows from committing oneself to action without delay. As you begin *right now*, you will act boldly, and others will see and respond to the genius, power, and magic within your actions.

Whatever you do, make it practical and useful. Too many talented people stall their productivity in waiting for the creative idea to gel or the transcendent idea to strike. Chances are not good that you will invent a new iPhone or the next generation of Facebook. But that does not mean that your product or service, empowered by your own genius, will not be successful. If your work meets practical needs, expect good results! Work even harder to drive those results to an entirely new level.

Remember that your ideas and work are not the total product. Take an appreciative look at each of the people who begin coming your way: customers, investors, potential colleagues, and even skeptical critics. Begin investing time and capital in those who can help take your work and run further with it than you have ever imagined. Appreciate these people and their gifts. Understand their desires and what they have to contribute. Hire them, sell to them, and dream further with them. Your work is valuable, but the people you work with might be far more important than your own beginning efforts.

Finally, work your initial idea through to its completion. Keep working until as many people as possible see the good results you are producing. Add value through advances and new versions of your initial product. And take some time to celebrate what you have done. It is important for everyone to see that you know you have done a great job.

CHAPTER 5

ENERGY FOR OUR WORK

IN ORDER TO really work, we need the opportunity to work (we need to be hired or to hire ourselves), we need a skill to put to work, and we need a significant amount of energy to throw into our work.

Energy is critical because without it, nothing much gets accomplished. We can show up, we can put in our hours, and we can even participate at a minimum level with coworkers in projects that look a bit like work. But without great amounts of personal energy, work goes nowhere. In fact, it is not even work; it is just time spent on the job.

Energy is the fuel for producing things. It is consumed and transformed into the refined and useful product of your work. Picture a block of wood in the hands of a carver. It is substantial, but it is unformed, plain, and lacking purpose, direction, and beauty. The wood carver needs a plan, and he needs the skill to remove parts of the wood to repurpose his resource as a useful, beautiful result. But what he really needs is the energy to throw into the task, otherwise work is reduced to just a plan—nothing is actually produced.

The carver's energy goes right to work. He chips away at corners and lightens the block to make a living, realistic image. He brings meaning to what was just a lump of unrealized potential. He does all this with purposeful cuts of his knife and slices of his chisel.

The workman does not hesitate. He has a plan and knows where he is going with his motions. Even when he seems to be destroying parts of the wood, he is re-forming the substance into true art. The block becomes a tool for future work or part of a larger project yet to be created.

The carver's energy burns inside him and translates itself into movements. He builds upon skilled motions and even invents with his mistakes. Everything he does is grist for the mill. Nothing gets wasted; all that is discarded adds to his purpose.

He bursts into action, followed by reflection. His pace is unpredictable. The workman owns his energy output and reaches down to find the strength he needs to produce something good. As a soldier's energy comes from a fit body and a good night's sleep, so a workman's energy comes from nourishing resources that have created his livelihood.

The carver's energy burns inside him and translates itself into movements. He builds upon skilled motions and even invents with his mistakes. Everything he does is grist for the mill.

Energy is always a bit elusive. When it is present, we feel its potential and see its results. But like the wind, we do not really see it! Yet energy is the real essence of work. We watch an athlete strain against his opponent; we see a body move, a pass being completed, a ball being batted, or a competitor claim victory. Energy works. As a mom trains her child to eat and dress himself, her energy is translated from skill into patience, movement, and love as she struggles with her child's accomplishments. The work seems to never end.

Where do we find this much-needed energy? The energy is already present within each of us. All of us can work. We must dig deep inside, sacrifice a bit of who we are, and then expend the energy we find. Remember, we are made to work, and we all have a reservoir of energy and talent to produce the important things of life: children, money, friendships, wonder, ideas, attitudes, and changed lives.

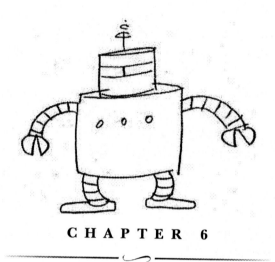

CHAPTER 6

IS IT FUN OR HARD WORK?

"Find a job you enjoy and you'll never work a day in your life!"

We've all heard that line before, and perhaps it is true. But it does presume a couple of important things. First, it assumes that you can enjoy your job all the time. I have enjoyed most of my jobs but not 90 percent of my working hours. There are always hard, troublesome parts of jobs. That is what work is about: doing hard things. Second, it assumes that we should not want to really work at all—just enjoy ourselves and get paid for it. Good-sounding gig, if you can get it. But it is not work.

Start with a realistic assumption: Work is hard (it is supposed to be hard; both God and your father promised you that). Work is also rewarding—financially, spiritually, physically, and socially. Expect work to be difficult, and expect it to pay.

Deal with the hard part first. People once struggled with horses and iron plows in frozen fields. We once rowed slow boats with heavy wooden oars. We once fought dirty and dangerous wars with explosives strapped to our shoulders. We still fight with troublesome ideas when we compose academic papers. We run into frustrating dead ends when we work to solve digital dilemmas for new software. We struggle to earn inflated sums of money needed for living expenses. And we fight to save a small portion of those earnings for the hard days ahead. Fair? Of course not. We do everything in our power to make work, clean, safe, simple, and easy—only to find it still difficult and complicated.

A successful career requires good education (college and professional degrees). Upon entering grad school in 1977, North Park Seminary's dean looked at my college transcript and said, "I see you did *your work* at Wheaton College." Work? What a thing for the dean to say! I was preparing for professional work, and the dean identified my college education as *my work*. He was right; college education was an important body of work to prepare me for seminary—to be followed by even more work. We are always working if we are investing ourselves in a positive direction and a course of preparation.

Work requires long hours—often our best hours. It may be twenty hours per week but more often forty to fifty-five hours per week. Add on commuting and special meetings. Work overwhelms everything else! I am now in my sixties. One of my jobs consumes twenty-five to thirty hours per week and the other fifteen to twenty hours. My workdays still stretch to eleven hours. Work does not seem to be slowing down!

Think back on when you worked the longest and hardest. Many long hours are not necessarily rewarding. They are simply long. And that is at least part of what work is about. Work means staying with the job until it is done. That may take twelve or even fourteen hours on a particular day. Accept it, and throw yourself into the job. You will get very tired. You will regather yourself and return to your work again.

With such an expenditure, you will need to schedule (or let your boss schedule) the proper and necessary rest. Aim for one or two days away from the office, driver's seat, factory, or classroom each week. Better to string two days together away (like a weekend!) than to take one day at a time. While I choose to work Saturday mornings, I enjoy a good recovery from Saturday afternoon until Monday afternoon. My wife and I recently enjoyed those two days away at the beautiful Gull Lake Retreat Center in Michigan. The energizing location made our two days feel like a week away. Water, woods, birds, new friends, and God's word all invaded my soul, refreshing my mind and body. After such a break, I can work again.

Work is hard on our muscles, our brains, and our relationships with people we love. It is also hard on our ability to come to terms with ourselves. That is what rest is all about—understanding and accepting who we are and how wonderfully we are created.

Work must be hard to produce intended and excellent results. Shoveling snow is hard work. You lift weight, you push slush, you breathe hard, and you sweat. This is what is all about—exertion, pain, recovery, and growth.

> *Work is hard on our muscles, our brains, and our relationships with people we love. It is also hard on our ability to come to terms with ourselves. That is what rest is all about—understanding and accepting who we are and how wonderfully we are created.*

You are an ER surgeon shuttling between patients. Your head, heart, and hands are all tired, and you still have a struggle ahead. This time it is a complex abdominal wound, and you have many stitches to complete. You are dead on your feet but you still must go on. People are counting on you to get everything done correctly. You are facing more than anyone should have to endure. You take a few sips of orange juice, summon up your will, say a quick prayer, and suit up for another set of incisions.

Your daughter Ellie needs help with her homework, but that will have to wait because you are the overscheduled mom who has to meet little Jason for his T-ball game. You get there but find the team's coach texting you—he has to work overtime and is asking you to manage the players for the next half hour. *"Please, not today!"* you insist. You have done school deliveries for the kids this morning; now it is a far-too-complicated afternoon. You are working at being a mom, chauffeur, cook, bookkeeper, and teacher. And now you are the substitute T-ball coach. You simply pull your ball cap a bit lower and get your kids through the first three innings.

These are all the hard sides of work. It draws on your energy and adds gray hairs. The extra work is worth it because you are investing that extra in people. Your work provides a kind of reward—a clean sidewalk, the sigh of relief when a husband sees his wife leave surgery, or the cheers of joy when your kid and eight others cross home plate with the first runs they have ever scored. It is all worthwhile.

The hours you invest at your job are supposed to be fulfilling, right? Certainly. Enjoy your work enough to provide the enthusiasm you need to earn your keep. And find a way to claim at least a couple of aspects of our job as *your own*.

I work in a garden center and have become the resident expert on soils, seeds, and peat moss. This means that I take on all customer questions regarding semi polluted urban soil. "You can grow both grass and gardenias," I exhort the people. Being an expert is fun. I like it when my customers listen to what I say and grow great grass. You see, I tend my own garden, and that validates much of what I tell my customers.

Invest personally in your work. If you do not enjoy your work, pick parts of your job and find two or three things at which you excel. Enjoy them immensely. It will make the boring minutes of your job more than tolerable.

Tailor your own work schedule toward your own enjoyment. The second half of my workday consists of writing and research. I love this work and can research things to death, but I won't. I will stop, write up my findings, and move on to more research. But I deliberately organize my favorite things toward the end of the workday—the 3:00–6:00 p.m. slot is my prime time for energy. Look out!

Early hours are the time for mandatory chores—the work that pays the bills. That is when I open the store, organize the flowers and fertilizers, clean and stock, set prices, and sell. A morning of chores is a reasonable price to pay to move on to my remaining hours of fulfillment. Always do the hard things first. The rest will take care of itself. A few more points on enjoying work:

1. Arrive for work on time. Continually organize your work hours and tasks. As you put your work on the clock, measure what counts and count all your production.
2. Produce all that is expected of you, and then produce some more. Seek to produce real products. Produce changes in the way you and others are working. Strive for quality and value in your work. Eliminate waste in time, energy, or resources.
3. Celebrate quitting time by completing all the tasks you can in a day. Then look forward to fulfillment in your remaining hours.
4. Enjoy the company of at least one other person at work, even if you stretch the day to fit that person into your hours. While I am much more a task person, I gain value

by receiving (questions, suggestions, etc.) from someone each day. Coworkers make my work better. Be interested in your boss; he or she needs attention as well. Be interested in the people whom other coworkers avoid. They bring value to your work.
5. Enjoy a small but healthy lunch midway through your workday. Think of it as a reward for what you have already accomplished. You are making a big investment of energy with each workday, and you need something tangible coming back to you. Build in a little bit of affirmation for all that you are sacrificing.

REAL PEOPLE: WORKING FOR GOD
RAY BAKKE—CITY PASTOR AND MISSIOLOGIST

Now in his late seventies, Ray Bakke grew up self-sufficient in Washington State. He learned to live broke but with hope for the future. He poured himself into reading, study, and God's call for his future as a Baptist minister. That call took him to Chicago's Moody Bible Institute, where he first learned the difference between reading and studying. He studied seriously, and he heard God's call to minister in the city.

As a young Chicago pastor, Ray adopted a formula for getting work done. "Divide the day into its natural three parts—morning, afternoon, and evening," Ray would say. "Work professionally two of those three segments; then work at home (recreationally) the other segment." While productive at both church and library, Ray proved to be even more creative in his work at home—with his family, right in their own neighborhood. He would develop effective urban-ministry strategies while helping his boys deliver newspapers or while commuting between far-flung Chicago seminaries. In effect, Ray was nearly always working. He just found practical ways to draw ideas from fast lunch conversations and generate productive friendships through academic pursuits. Ray's life and work fused into a unified, self-propagating whole. Preaching and teaching produced both ideas and smiles, and more smiles gathered even more people to his never-ending causes.

BILL BRIGHT—CANDY MAKER, CAMPUS EVANGELIST, MISSION EXECUTIVE

Oklahoma-born candy maker Bill Bright was never one to shy away from hard work—making batches, filling orders, and prospering in a tough business for small companies. But he was also spiritually restless. He searched the Bible to find both meaning and calling. After surrendering his life to Jesus and moving to California, Bright began studies first at Princeton and then at Fuller Theological Seminary. He became an evangelist (organizing Christian outreach on the UCLA campus in 1951) and a mission executive (building Campus Crusade into the world's largest Christian mission agency).

Never known for creativity, Bright focused his energy and spiritual passion on production and growth in campus evangelism. He always set ambitious numerical goals for Campus Crusade and often succeeded in exceeding those marks. His landmark accomplishments include (1) gathering of more than one hundred thousand young people for Explore '72 in Dallas, Texas; (2) production and distribution of the Jesus Film Project in the 1980s and '90s; and (3) establishment of two large headquarters and retreat centers for Campus Crusade—first in San Bernardino, California, and then in Orlando, Florida. Bill Bright's legacy lives on with Cru—Campus Crusade's successor agency impacting Christian mission on every continent.

TODAY'S WORKERS: JANE, JACKIE, GEORGE, TIM

Jane Quigley and Jackie Quinn are half-sisters who have gotten along better than most siblings ever would. They and their kids, Aiden and Melissa, each from previous marriages, live together in one large house with George Williams and Tim Franchelli—each of whom are parents to two elementary school girls: Jennie and Millie, and Louisa and Elsa. It is a total of ten people, with four adult wage earners.

Everyone likes each other well enough, but money is the force binding them together. They enjoy a nice old house on East Avenue in cozy Oak Park, Illinois, with lots of bedrooms and storage. And while each adult works at a downtown, middle-class job, no one would be able to independently provide the good standard of living that they can all enjoy together.

While this complicated living plan seems to work well for this East Avenue clan, the household budget remains tight. Not one of the adults or their kids feel that they are getting rich, but they are glad to get by in a comfortable fashion in the near-city Oak Park community.

Jane and Jackie have lived together in Oak Park nearly all their lives, other than the four years they each invested in short-lived marriages. The sisters put together the idea of a shared household to make ends meet but also to have some go-to guys (the men) around the house who loved housework and all the hard jobs!

George Williams was an old college friend of the sisters from DePaul University days, who five years ago broached the idea of his old graduate-school buddy Tim Franchelli moving in with his two girls. These guys work hard, put their energy into home up-keep, and leave little elbowroom for others in the kitchen. Truth be told, their two mini-families dominate the household work.

To make finances work, every adult needs to pitch in $1,000 monthly for household food and entertainment budget and $2,500 monthly to the house account—mortgage, taxes, utilities, insurance, maintenance, major repairs, and legal costs. All four adults are co-owners of the East Avenue home, and each has the option of cashing out their stake and nominating new resident owners upon six months' notice.

Without the hefty monthly investment of each owner, the house could not be maintained. Each owner must work at full capacity at their weekday job and sometimes find an extra source of income for savings, auto, entertainment, and vacation. It's tricky and demanding! But it allows everyone to enjoy a better lifestyle than anyone could by themselves.

Jane works full time in the Cook County's Assessor's Office—her job routine but remarkably profitable. Her commute to downtown Chicago is easy and cheap, allowing her to forgo owning a car. Jackie also has a stable career in development at her alma mater, DePaul University. The university dominates her social life and will provide her a good future. She is a Chicagoan for life.

George earns well over $100K most years at the Chicago Mercantile Exchange. But he also has some big losses and major child support expenses (his two sons live with his ex-wife). He likes the Oak Park home and occasionally must do extra tax work to support his lifestyle and commitments.

Tim does well in commercial accounts for Chicago-based Northern Trust Company. His income exceeds $120K, but he too has child support payments and educational loans from grad school. Tim also spends a lot on winter and summer golf vacations—something he cannot live without!

Jane, Jackie, George, and Tim all seem to be doing well with their shared-cost household but changing demands loom for each one of them.

On a whim, George and Tim accepted their friend Larry's invitation to a flip-that-house lunch presentation. They didn't expect much except a reunion lunch with their old college buddy at the downtown Marriott. They enjoyed the event and the speaker's challenge. It was enough to get George, Tim, and Larry scrapping together cash for a few residential investments. Together the three had enough funds to put 25 percent down on a twelve-unit apartment building in Chicago's trendy Kenwood neighborhood. They quickly became good landlords and found themselves collecting about $2,100 per month on each of the twelve apartments. Taxes, roof repairs, and new wiring were considerable expenses. But the three guys toughed it out and after two years made more money as landlords than they thought possible.

George and Tim agreed to try more building investments. George stayed with the Kenwood area, purchasing an old, well-kept eight-unit building. Tim decided that he could extend his finances close to home in Oak Park with a large twenty-four-unit efficiency apartment building. Each unit brought in about $1,100 per month and occupied every bit of Tim's free time in cleaning, repairs, rental showings, and a few troublesome evictions. He had not bargained for all this, but he found that he was doing better with the Oak Park building than the three-way investment in Kenwood. Owning and renting had become almost another full-time job, and it paid better than his day job.

In talking things over at Starbucks a few months later, George and Tim realized that as single guys with limited family responsibilities, they had gotten into real estate just to explore their own money-making abilities. They had done well, but now after three years of trying things out, they were ready to make some big moves—more than just making money. They were each approaching age forty, and they needed to put down anchors and raise new families of their own.

George had been seeing Vanessa at a church singles group, right in Oak Park. Tim also visited the singles group and met Julie—a thirty-six-year-old single mom with three kids. New relationships proved to be the right move for everyone. Neither George nor Tim is prone to push his way around, but they are builders concerned with what they can give to others.

After a year of getting to know each other, George and Vanessa told her three children as well as George's children of their decision to get married. It complicates life, holidays, and relationships for both, but it also completes life for them. They have found great friends in an adult fellowship at Oak Park's Calvary Church—people who will be the center of a strong family support group for years to come. George and Vanessa are planning wisely; their wedding date is ten months ahead—time enough to stabilize work, secure good housing, and get to know each other's friends and family. While they are doing well financially, they know they will have bigger responsibilities in the years ahead.

Tim and Julie are taking things a bit slower, which works just fine for them and their families. Real estate continues to occupy a big part of life as Tim's second-income stream, and now Julie has decided to join him in property ownership. She has realized that her own organizational and people skills can be put to good use, making money and discovering what motivates Tim. Julie knew she had met a great guy, but she did not realize how possessed Tim could be when it came to properties and housing. Tim and Julie are learning to make money together in their part-time business, but they are also learning what people who have been through divorces, medical disasters, or even the death of a spouse need most. When they finally decide on marriage for themselves, they will be well schooled in the life nuances they need to understand.

This much Tim and Julie know: when you form a meaningful relationship, you must say good-bye to some previous commitments but keep in close touch with the jobs that provide good streams of income. At present, Tim continues to live at the East Avenue house while his growing relationship with Julie moves him in a new direction for the future. George has packed his things, married, and found a new future with Vanessa and her family in suburban Glen Ellyn. It was tough saying good-bye to his housemates on East Avenue, but they each know that they have built solid friendships for the future.

Tim and Julie are learning to make money together in their part-time business, ... When they finally decide on marriage for themselves, they will be well schooled in the life nuances they need to understand.

Jane and Jackie continue to build their careers and their steady Oak Park lives. Granted, they feel financially nervous with George moving out and with Tim's expected move in the next year. But both Jane and Jackie are realistic about the need for change and financial shifts. They have already begun interviewing potential residential owners for their cohousing arrangements. In combining contacts from their old schools, workplaces, and local churches, Jane and Jackie have built a list of ten good candidates. And they realize their plan of four resident owners could be expanded to six. New income streams are always important. The East Avenue house is big enough to handle many people, and interest in cohousing is stronger than either Jane or Jackie previously realized. Everyone is learning lessons from their dynamic set of work and life arrangements:

1. Work hard, develop a second stream of income, minimize extraordinary household expenses, and plan for the long term while expecting change at any time.
2. Have faith in the future. It usually rewards productive workers and mentally tough individuals.
3. Be ready to change and grow no matter how content you may feel. Change will be hard, but it will be rewarding if you love well, work hard, and plan carefully.

CHAPTER 7

WORK: YOUR INHERITANCE

WE LIKE OPTIONS, and we have grown to demand good options to what were once thought to be givens in life. We are even growing to be a culture of great options in our work lives. While a person may be skilled and successful at his accounting job, he can still decide to take a year off as a sabbatical or even retrain for a new career.

But work itself is not an option for a person who has a healthy view of God, a healthy view of himself, and a realistic view of his own place in history. We humans were created to work—to be creative stewards of the world and its resources. Face it: we are hardwired to work. Laziness is really a practiced rebellion against the production ethic that was built into us at creation and has been practiced for generations.

Start with your own family and ask these questions: Who were your grandfathers? Who were your grandmothers? My grandfathers were painters and tool- and diemakers (I still have some of Ted Johnson's old tools). These occupations were major parts of their lives. That does not mean that Ted Johnson just chipped away at steel slabs every day. He was also a fruit picker, a salesman, and a great husband, father, and neighbor. We all do varieties of things in order to survive and thrive. But inevitably, our occupations form an identity around us.

We humans were created to work—to be creative stewards of the world and its resources.

While I have worked at a variety of specific jobs, the employer who has known me best sees me as essentially a researcher. I love to sort through history, background, and details. I love to dig deep and then present facts in such a way that present-day leaders can make healthy and intelligent decisions. It is freeing and empowering for me to know myself as a researcher. Knowing that identity and building my best work around it, I can then go on to do a great job at any number of tasks that I am given.

We are all workers. Our parents worked at specific jobs, and their parents worked at specific jobs as well. Ancestors from generations back had to work to pay for living expenses, raise their children, contribute to their communities, and fulfill their God-given expectations. We have inherited this role as worker because we are human. To be human is to work.

God (a person himself) is a worker: creating the universe, building relationships with his created people, sacrificing for grand purposes, sustaining the world, and forgiving and redeeming humans who have strayed in their own ways. God is now working to build new homes for past, present, and future generations of his children.

We are God's offspring in the sense that all humanity has a bit of God's image created within us. God has *inspired* us or breathed into us some of himself at our own creation. Human birth is more than biological reproduction. It is God's chance to once again create a human soul with his own stamp on it.

CHAPTER 8

MONEY, DEBT, SAVING

WHEN WE WORK, we make money. If we do not make enough money, then part of our work is to fix that financial end of the bargain. Volunteering is great, but it is not the real work that we have been called to engage in. Your employer has got to have some skin in the game.

So what do we do with all the money we earn? Lots of it goes to pay for the basic costs of living: rent or mortgage, food, medical costs, transportation, clothes, utilities, and taxes of all kinds. Many of us have outstanding debts or loans to pay off. And sometimes, it seems that we pay and pay, without ever getting those car loans, college loans, back taxes, or child support totally taken care of. Paying debts seems like another job that always confronts us.

The best advice comes in advance: do not pile up debts in the first place. The advice of the New Testament is "Owe no man anything" (Rom. 13:8), which hardly seems realistic in our credit-card, debt-driven world. Yet the meaning of the biblical writer's words remains vivid: Owe creditors as little as possible if you really want to follow Jesus. The Bible is quite realistic about the power of money (particularly borrowed money) in our lives.

So what do we do with debts—paralyzing student loans of over $80,000 or a nagging credit-card balance that just will not fall below $2,000? Pay them off quickly; or if you are fortunate enough, immediately. It may be necessary to develop a firm, long-range plan for paying off nagging debts. Whatever plan it takes, establish it and stick to it. Financial debts are the economic fat cells stealing years of healthy living and eventually killing you.

Two years into our marriage, Ruth and I bought our first home and quickly spent thousands of dollars that we did not have on good and necessary-looking home repairs. Our cozy workers' cottage was a hundred-year-old home, and many windows and doors needed replacing. Our beginning $200 credit-card balance quickly rose to $8,000, then $9,000, and finally just over $11,000. We were both working forty-hour jobs, though we needed to be paid better by our employers. Still, we had to do something swift and effective to pay off Visa and curtail our out-of-control spending. We did both.

Ruth and I promised each other that we would pay Visa $1,000 each month, beginning that October 1994, until we had taken the balance down to zero, some fifteen months later. We also removed our VISA cards out of our wallets and placed them in a dresser drawer we seldom used. We promised each other that we would begin using a designated amount of cash each week for groceries and transportation. If we needed to use our credit card for a special and important purchase, we would first consult each other, explaining and justifying the purchase. Most of the time, our requests were unjustifiable wishes. We soon recognized that and decided to live without the purchase before even raising it as a request. We learned that we could easily live without a theater ticket, a restaurant meal, or even use of a car (plus insurance and gas) for six months. We did a lot of walking and cooking at home in our refurbished kitchen. Life was simple and good that year and for several years to follow.

Yes, we did kill off the $11,000 debt, and we have not paid a great amount of interest to credit-card companies in more than twenty-two years. We learned the reality of living within our means, even during times when we were unemployed. Credit-card debts and compound interest in excess of 18 percent or 26 percent are simply a penalty not worth paying. The joy of deferred gratification (paying in full with cash in hand) became a delight that we have never gotten over.

When debts are paid off and spending is reined in to living within one's means, individuals and families have the joy of saving for the future. Is this the kind of stewardship of one's resources that the Bible has in mind when it calls us God's stewards of the resources he has given us? You bet it is!

Saving is a joy and privilege but also a difficult challenge. Most of us are would-be savers and undisciplined spenders at the very same time. Household economics includes much in the way of gray areas. The goal is to become less and less a spender and more and more a saver—always with God's future tied to our own future.

Spend smart and spend together (husbands and wives). Accountability tied to the person you love and the people you care for reins in our selfish desires. Who is most frugal—you or your spouse? The most frugal person should keep the checkbook, assuming he or she is a good accountant!

That same person should also be in charge of savings—writing checks to yourselves for reserve accounts, IRAs, stocks, life insurance, and paying the mortgage (double payments are always a good strategy).

Everyone needs to get excited about saving. You are making a deposit for your future. It is a way to improve (maybe even extend) the quality of your life. And it is also a great way to give to the people you love and the institutions that share your values. Saving and investing are the ways we celebrate the good values that we have worked out through our life efforts. Yes, life is uncertain. But saving for the future is bound to succeed in even the most unlikely circumstances.

Everyone needs to get excited about saving. You are making a deposit for your future. It is a way to improve (maybe even extend) the quality of your life.

Arthur Johnson was never a successful man by usual estimates. My uncle Art lived on the margins of life, spending most of his adult years in Veterans' Administration institutions, plagued by frequent seizures and illnesses. But Uncle Art had worked and saved for six years prior to World War II, putting away thousands of dollars that were never touched by medical needs. He had no occasion to spend any of these funds. Upon his death in 1989, my brother and I were fortunate to be recipients of his estate. The money I received from Uncle Art enabled me to take a life-changing trip to Norway, Sweden, and Russia. I was welcomed and transformed by meeting Arthur Johnson's relatives in Sweden. My world grew bigger, and I found larger meaning in the families God had created for me. I saw Russia explode with democratic energy and optimism. I came home a new man, ready to marry my fiancée Ruth and begin a new life with her. Uncle Art never married, never owned a home, never built a career, and never lived a fulfilled life. Those *nevers* plagued him into his senior years. But he did earn and save money during his twenties, and his savings enabled me to expand and restart my own life in 1990. Few of us will ever know the greatest parts of our legacy. Art Johnson never did. But he worked, saved, and blessed the people he loved most.

My world grew bigger, and I found larger meaning in the families God had created for me.

REAL PEOPLE: HARD WORKERS
BERNIE HELGESEN—RAILROADER, PILOT, CAPITALIST

My uncle, Bernhard Helgesen, grew up poor in Chicago during 1930s. But he never accepted things as they were. He tried new tasks and invented jobs others never saw coming. When the Pacific War raged in the 1940s, Bernie enlisted right at his seventeenth birthday. While battling on the ocean, he was captivated by fast fighter planes. Upon returning home, he earned his pilot's license by age twenty.

For Bernie, romance was in the skies; but real money was to be made on the rails. Without a high-school diploma (he completed that years later), Bernie began his career as a Milwaukee Road conductor: commuter runs from Elgin, Illinois, to downtown Chicago. Capitalizing on numerous friendships, Bernie (and his wife Pat) raised five boys, bought homes, boats, planes, and even a farm in Arkansas. But he wanted more than his daily commuter runs divided by a four-hour layover in Chicago's Loop. Bernie talked his way onto the trading floor at the Chicago Board of Trade—buying low, selling high, and saving all he earned. Commodities trading became a second-income stream, and soon real estate became a third. While juggling business pursuits, Bernie Helgesen thought of himself as a pilot, sailor, whittler, and farmer. He loved the air, water, trees, and soil, working hard and profiting in each place.

WAYNE KISER—EDITOR, WRITER, PRINTER, PREACHER

Wayne Kiser was raised to be a worker in Traverse City, Michigan. His commitment to Jesus, his studies at Moody Bible Institute, and his drive to communicate the gospel through written words drove him to be a printer, graphic artist, author, preacher, and magazine editor. During the 1960s, Wayne and his wife, Ruth

Ann, founded Graphic & Editorial Services in Glen Ellyn, Illinois. Wayne's love for all things mechanical was displayed in his basement and garage filled with printing presses, folding machines, bindery machines, and even old Studebakers. While he loved to collect things that worked, he loved even more to produce effective Christian publications: brochures, magazines, books, and ground-breaking websites.

For nearly fifty years, Wayne and Ruth Ann produced phenomenal quantities of missions and Christian-education materials. Their ten- and twelve-hour workdays impacted the lives of thousands of people who will never know the Kiser name. Just as well for Wayne Kiser. Why get caught up with honors and awards when you can reach down deep inside yourself to serve Jesus and his followers?

TODAY'S WORKER: CHARLEY—OFF AND RUNNING

Charley will graduate from East Valley Community College next month with an associate's degree in Digital Media Production. It sounds good, but he knows that two years of higher education does not put him high on anyone's achievement list. He needs to get a degree in something worthwhile, and it has got to earn him some real money.

At age twenty, Charley has been going to school (in some form or another) for a long time. He is an expert in attending classes, taking tests, and writing papers. But he has never sold a graphic design, negotiated a contract, or produced a TV commercial. Charley has been too busy studying to do any real work. He has made a few thousand dollars parking cars at East Valley music events, and he has waited tables at the ski resort up in the mountains. He is beginning to dream about what he is going to do with his first $35K salary.

While all his best friends at East Valley have already been accepted as degree students at State Polytechnic or Millhouse University, Charley is getting interested in taking a year off studies and kick-starting his career in sales and marketing. In the past two weeks, he has completed three job interviews at valley area FM stations, including one at the growing public radio station now housed at State Poly.

Fast forward a month and Charley has not only earned his associate's degree but also landed the assistant audio-tech job at State Poly's KSPU. At forty thousand watts, the station reaches a young audience in three states and will give Charley a chance to hone his skills with a $2,400 per month starting salary. He will bike to work, live cheap in student apartments, and work long hours—absorbing everything he can about the digital bits and quirks of radio sound production.

In a matter of weeks, Charley has moved from student to worker, from reading to real money. He is scared and delighted at all the next several weeks will hold: no summer vacation, late night hours, and responsibilities he is not ready to handle. It is a crash course in real life!

Shift ahead three months and Charley finds himself excited about all he's doing and earning. He likes living cheap and saving $400 each pay period. At this rate, he'll put away nearly $8,000 by next summer. He never realized life could be this profitable.

In a matter of weeks, Charley has moved from student to worker, from reading to real money.

In bigger ways, Charley has grown beyond his classroom experiences. He now sees a purpose to the hard work of future study. Within another year, he will apply as a transfer student to State Poly's Digital Media program while continuing work at KSPU-FM. His work will fuel his studies while professors will hone his academic skills. As work and school harmonize, Charley will discover extra meaning in all he does. His final two years of bachelor's studies will be an accelerated course in life success. In addition, the contacts he makes through station personnel, professors, and students will fill out his media experience in rich ways.

And his decision to work and go to school is responsible for this profit, confidence, and future. Charley's life is off and running.

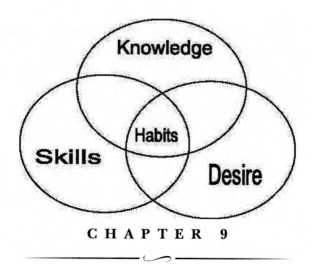

CHAPTER 9

GET MOVING: MAKING WORK A HABIT

VERY LITTLE HAPPENS without motion. Even the stabilizing of gravity begins by pulling us in a strong, powerful direction. Movement and activity are essential to starting and finishing worthwhile projects. If you are standing still, you have very little chance of finding your work. But if you are moving—between people, places, generations, and styles—you have a good chance to discover your work and do that work.

A FEW NECESSITIES FOR MOTION:
Sleep—Yes, you need to rest (and rest well!) to move effectively. Do not be afraid of at least seven (probably eight) hours of sleep each night. Nothing gets us ready for ideas, service, and motion better than sleep.

If you are standing still, you have very little chance of finding your work. But if you are moving—between people, places, generations, and styles—you have a good chance to discover your work and do that work.

Direction—Without a map, you will not know where you are going. Make your daily and weekly agenda your motion map. As you create an agenda and follow it, you will see the meaning behind that map emerging. Your directions soon become indispensable tools for living and moving. As author Steven Covey (*The Seven Habits of Highly Effective People*) repeated often, "Plan tomorrow today." You will find plans to be grounding, liberating, and empowering.

Energy—Insist on operating at full energy to put yourself in motion for work. If you need to eat better (healthy fruits and vegetables, less sugar and fat), start right now. If you need an exercise and fitness plan, develop it and begin practicing it. If you are stuck on addictive substances that sap your energy, make changes in those unhealthy habits as soon as possible. You will need every bit of energy that you can find.

Intentionality—Do not count on anything happening by accident. It is great when you discover a new friend or resource by happenstance. But those accidents happen rarely. Make your own moves with every intention of them paying off. Know your intent for every hour you invest, every personal visit, or every interview you conduct. Plan your coffee breaks with a purpose in mind. Succeed at the game of intentionality.

Courage—Almost every move in life takes a bit of courage. Moving often means going from a familiar place (or experience) to a very different place. Some moves are scary enough to paralyze your will unless you have armed yourself with a needed supply of courage. And where do you get it? Consider three sources: (a) borrow some courage from friends—spend time with brave, forward-thinking people, (b) buy a bit of courage through a class or conference, or (c) grow your own supply of courage by practice and reflection on making hard decisions.

Start without thinking! —The most difficult act in all of sports is hitting a baseball thrown at over ninety-five miles per hour. Even the best hitters succeed only about 35 percent of the time. And the best hitters all agree on this—"Don't think too much!" If you want to get moving and do something hard, do not waste time thinking about it—just do it!

Go with your instinct—When you are just starting out and you really do not know which move is best to make, trust your instincts and go with your best hunch. Instincts eliminate the energy waste accompanying overthinking and worrying, and they often lead to good decisions. When you do not have either the time or capacity to think something through, go with what your gut tells you, and you will be surprised how far that decision takes you.

Create Motion:

Begin new habits—With no suggestion or permission, begin a healthy new habit today. Scientists tell us that it takes about twenty-one days to form and set a habit. Enjoy salads for lunch. Walk thirty minutes each day. Memorize classic poetry. Practice calculus. The point is to begin something new, healthy, and challenging. There is no substitute for beginning right now!

Claim your mission—Think of something you would like to make a part of your life mission. Claim it now, make it yours, and own it. It is one thing to do a good deed for your neighborhood by cleaning up a garbage-strewn lot. But you make it your mission when you buy that lot and determine to clean, maintain, and beautify it. Ownership changes everything! Put your money on the line, and make things happen.

Meet new people—Determine to meet new people, up to five more people each month than you do usually. Stretch your personality and watch how your new acquaintances begin expanding your life. You will move faster and go farther.

Find accountability partners—Not many, perhaps one or two people will do just fine. A group of three will keep you accountable to your goals and keep you moving ahead.

Break old habits—As you build new habits and begin moving in new directions, some old habits (perhaps a bad habit) will have to go. There is simply no room for them in your motion-filled life. Do not get too hung up on poor habits that plague your present life. Guilt is a relatively poor motivator. Simply move ahead with your good habits, and determine to filter the bad ones out. Start sorting and prioritizing. Old habits will disappear.

Make motion natural—As you practice forward movement, work to make greater motion a natural part of your existence. Look for ways to work efficiently. Get curious and solve problems. Move ahead easily and naturally. Legendary basketball coach John Wooden told his players at UCLA, "Be quick but don't hurry." After weeks of building quickness into your routine, very little about you will be unnaturally hurried. Expect motion in your life, and you will easily create it.

As you practice forward movement, work to make greater motion a natural part of your existence. Look for ways to work efficiently. Get curious and solve problems. Move ahead easily and naturally.

DIRECT YOUR MOTION:
Motion is necessary, but in itself it is not enough. Each of us can move in many directions, stuffing our agendas full. But we may still be headed nowhere in particular. Take time to determine, set,

and measure your own life direction. When you establish solid and visible direction, you understand the purpose of your movements.

Momentum—The Tool We All Need:

A fast, strong 180-pound skier begins his course at a standstill. Determining his goal to ski his first mile in five minutes and then another two miles in the next nine minutes, he begins his fluid, almost effortless motions. As he gains speed, he is not working harder. He is working smarter and more efficiently. He finds the trail's shortcut down a gentle hill and begins using gravity to his advantage. The next time down the course, he waxes his skis and finds the magical power of momentum working to his advantage. As the skier's confidence, courage, and skill grow, he realizes that he cannot be stopped. He defeats inertia and discovers an invisible engine all his own. None of us can excel simply by our own effort. But as we discover the power of momentum, we use every bit of its magic to our advantage.

Start Right Now—Begin:

Sure ways to sabotage work and movement:

- Overthink something or anything! Try doing first, and then evaluating later.
- Worry about your first move—even what to do with your initial success.
- Make an exhaustive list—needs, schedules, purchases, rules…please no!
- Ask every smart question you can think of—not so smart at all.
- Dream of either failure or what you will do with success. Stay right in the moment.

When your alarm clock rings, get right up. When your laptop lights up, begin typing. When a person asks you a question, respond (even if you have to plead ignorance). If you are the first to tee off, one practice swing is more than enough; hit the ball. Thinking too long can be deadly. Trust your first impression, and run with it. You may do things differently the second and third time through, but you will be glad you first trusted your instincts and skills.

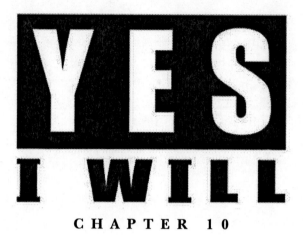

CHAPTER 10

ACCEPT WORK

WORK IS WHAT we do; we are made tough enough to handle it and sensitive enough to appreciate its rewards. As far back as 1995, in his prophetic book *The End of Work*, economist Jeremy Rifkin argued that we were entering a new phase in history—one characterized by a steady decline of jobs. "The world," said Rifkin, "is fast polarizing into two potentially irreconcilable forces: on one side, an information elite that controls and manages the high-tech global economy; and on the other, the growing numbers of displaced workers, who have few prospects and little hope for meaningful employment in an increasingly automated world." In his 2002 book, *The Rise of the Creative Class*, urban theorist Richard Florida told us that future cities would succeed by attracting knowledge workers. He argued that creative thinking, technical knowledge, and specific skills had become the raw materials and currency upon which urban America would thrive.

Two decades later we have found out just how right Rifkin, Florida, and other late twentieth-century thinkers really were.

The Great Recession (2007–2011) spelled the end for many workers and the marginalization of many others. While a host of traditional jobs have disappeared, work itself continues to stare us in the face. God ordained work, and our economic survival depends upon it. Work remains a challenge to all of us.

We are Created for Work

At God's creation of our world, humans were assigned the role of "workers in his vineyard" (Matthew 20:2, NIV). While historians and Bible scholars used to see work as a curse (resulting from human sin), a closer examination of the Genesis account shows that people were given specific tasks even before the fall.

Genesis 2:8 and 2:15 (NIV) tell us, "Now the Lord God had planted a garden in the east, in Eden; and there he put the man he had formed. The Lord God took the man and put him in the Garden of Eden to work it and take care of it." Immediately upon creation of the man (Adam), God has assigned him the job of taking care of the perfectly created Garden of Eden. Adam was given the tasks of tending trees, growing fruits, and caring for rivers. Our original ancestor had several original occupations: horticulturalist, farmer, and marine biologist.

Genesis 2:19–20a (NIV) tells us, "Now the Lord God had formed out of the ground all the wild animals and all the birds in the sky. He brought them to the man to see what he would name them; and whatever the man called each living creature, that was its name. So the man gave names to all the livestock, the birds in the sky and all the wild animals." Another part of Adam's work was to name the animals God had created—both domestic and wild. In naming the animals, Adam is exercising dominion and authority over the animals—a God-given privilege and task. God gave Adam this responsibility to establish human supremacy over the animal kingdom.

God has described humans by their work ever since. The genealogies of Genesis 4 identify Cain as "builder of a city," Jubal as "the father of all who play stringed instruments and pipes," and Tubal-Cain as one who "forged tools out of bronze and iron." Clearly these early people were known by their abilities and their work.

The Limits of Leisure

Today's human focus rests increasingly upon fulfilment, joy, pleasure, and leisure. We desire to become greater persons through expanding our lifestyles and activities. My Sunday *Chicago Tribune* includes sections on real estate, romance, travel, restaurants, television, and even the comics. The weekly message lands with a thud on my doorstep—have fun, develop yourself, live to be a hundred, enjoy a better sex life, be interesting and witty, and do not let work and achievement get the best of you.

Leisure is necessary to renew our energies and provide space for reflection, innovation, and worship. But our present generation has transformed leisure into an excuse for license, pride, and laziness. Often, leisure is practiced as a pseudo vocation. Travel itineraries have become new versions of daily work schedules. Fitness fanatics spend their time at gyms, spas, beaches, and ski slopes. These people are enjoying life, but they are missing out on work as a God-given element. They are not using their energies to produce a product or change a static reality.

> **Leisure is necessary to renew our energies and provide space for reflection, innovation, and worship. But our present generation has transformed leisure into an excuse for license, pride, and laziness.**

Leisure, healthy as it is, does not end in a product or a changed world view. When we work, we invest our energies in producing something—either tangible or conceptual. Work makes a difference in both our lives and the world around us.

Leisure provides a break from the routines of work (positive or negative); it refreshes and renews our spirits, bodies, and minds. But leisure does have its limits. It empowers and enlarges us, but it does not produce the results of genuine work.

Coming to Terms with Work

Work has taken on a negative meaning in recent decades. Once thought to be a calling, work has become an assigned job, drudgery, or even punishment. Granted, some aspects of work may never be fulfilling. Commuting has become a tiresome and expensive part of the job for many Americans. Woody Allen offered some wisdom when he famously said, "Ninety percent of life is just showing up."

Coming to terms with work simply means that we accept and even delight in our work enough to keep coming back to it when our work is draining as well as when it is delightful.

If we are to understand and enjoy the benefits of work, we must first come to terms with all that work is and is not.

- Work is not a break or vacation. Work is our effort and time spent fully engaged with products, tools, people, ideas, or resources that can be changed or improved upon.
- Work is not a distraction from the main idea at hand. Work is the main event that dominates our attention for productive purposes.
- Work takes large amounts of our energy—though it should not destroy or defeat us. Humans must invest

themselves in work and be rewarded for their efforts to return to productive work again and again.
- Work provides us with goals, rewards, praise, learning, and satisfaction.
- Work leaves us with the sense and knowledge that we have accomplished a part of what God has created us for as human beings.
- Work should provide us with money and material resources. Your present salary may not be what you deserve, but it should provide a financial base fundamental to your notion of work.

Coming to terms with work simply means that we accept and even delight in our work enough to keep coming back to it when our work is draining as well as when it is delightful. When we understand that our work has both costs and rewards and we keep investing time and energy in new avenues for work, then we are truly coming to terms with our work.

CHAPTER 11

PREPARE FOR WORK

THIS MUCH WE know:

- People are called to meaningful work.
- Like money, gainful employment is scarce.
- We face a challenging task in preparing for the job that will pay the wage we need and deserve.

Preparing for profitable work is crucial work in and of itself. Nobody falls into a good job (let along the right job!) these days. Preparation includes physical conditioning, acquiring work ethic and accompanying habits, making the right choices, and pursuing general education. It is all part of the work that we do. Let's prepare.

PHYSICAL CONDITIONING
It may not be the Tour de France, but your chosen job means eight to ten hours each day of top-level focus and function. It demands both physical preparation and health maintenance.

If you are fighting an illness, win most of that fight before you begin a new job. You will get off on the right foot and establish excellent work habits from the outset. Start a healthy sleep pattern. Get to bed early for seven to eight hours of sleep each night, and wake up thirty minutes earlier than you need to for your shower, breakfast, and commute. You will need a half hour for planning the day, directing your soul, and taking care of small emergencies.

If you are not already exercising, start a fitness program of 3–4 workout sessions each week. Schedule outdoor walks frequently at noon or after work. As more work locks us indoors, it is increasingly important to move briskly and breathe fresh air for 30–90 minutes daily.

Eat well but not too much! Major in breakfast—fruits and grains. Orange juice and extra vitamin C will get you through the toughest weather. Watch your calorie intake and maintain a lean physique—five pounds lighter in summer is a good rule of thumb. Let your physical condition work to your advantage, and you will have no need to call in sick as Thursday drags into Friday.

Acquiring a Work Ethic

We tend to think of work as doing one difficult thing after another until our cumulative impact validates us as a good worker. That may have been true at one point in history but no longer. Work requires a preexisting ethic, setting us on a course to do the following:

- Show up expecting to produce and be useful.
- Expect change because of your work efforts.
- Demand growth and/or profit resulting from your work.
- Enjoy and thrive on both the value and results of work.

It was once said, "You're not supposed to enjoy it; that's why they call it work!" Work has a long history of being a series of painful, tiring, and exhausting efforts resulting in economic benefit for an individual but little else in terms of satisfaction, enjoyment, and productive achievement for the greater society.

Even most of our artistic efforts to celebrate work have ended up as bitter lament of the hardship and personal drain for little money or meaning. In the 1950s Nashville crooner Tennessee Ernie Ford sang,

> "You load sixteen tons, what do you get, another day older and deeper in debt. Saint Peter, don't you call me 'cause I can't go, I owe my soul to the company store."

By the 1990s, Dolly Parton was singing,

> "Working 9 to 5, what a way to make a living, barely getting by. It's all taking and no giving. They just use your mind, and they never give you credit. It's enough to drive you crazy if you let it. 9 to 5, for service and devotion, you would think that I would deserve a fair promotion, want to move ahead but the boss won't seem to let me. I swear sometimes that man is out to get me."

A bit more comedy and a bit less physical drudgery but work remains the same: no credit, not enough money, and little rewards. There has got to be something more in it for all of us.

> **Even most of our artistic efforts to celebrate work have ended up as bitter lament of the hardship and personal drain for little money or meaning.**

To find meaning in work, start by building a work ethic that can carry you through even the bitter times of daily work. The tasks we are forced to do may not always be rewarding, but each of us still owns the right to choose our attitude toward our work. Choose the work ethic that says the following:

- I will carry out every task in a complete and excellent fashion.
- I will learn from and process the work experience in order to become skilled, wise, and experienced.
- I will seek work in which I can:
  - produce greatly;
  - serve myself, the people around me, and my God;
  - excel and mentor others in how to work effectively and productively.

Why an ethic regarding work? It is a fair question! Because human work is sacred. We earn money, we produce goods, and we serve our community. But even beyond those important things, our work is ordained by God. God calls us to be stewards and workers even when our work is difficult. Just as God creates us to be his human beings, so he calls us to work, tend, and produce.

Choosing Suitable and Profitable Work

As we watch the various ways in which people spend their working hours, we are forced to ask, "What really is suitable and profitable work for me?" It was once quite satisfactory (and profitable) to continue in the vocation established by one's parents: Father and Son Pizza, Lever Brothers, Lundberg Family Farms. Those options may now be quaint, few, and forgotten. But we have the chance to carve out better ways of finding and entering suitable lines of work.

Pursuing General Education for Work

Mostly all work now requires thinking, diligence, concentration, and follow-through. In general education (secondary school and most of one's college education), seek to become a clear, sharp, and concise thinker. Learn to understand words (also sentences and paragraphs) and their complete meaning. Learn to converse, following the flow of every conversation you are part of and some you eavesdrop on. Add to the quality of the conversation rather than inserting opinions and pithy statements. Listen and understand people: their wishes, intents, values, and emotions—oftentimes their unspoken words. Learn to follow leaders' orders and become a good leader yourself, adopting the best that great leaders offer.

REAL PEOPLE: COMMITTED WORKERS
HERMAN MUELLER–METALLURGIST AND BLACKSMITH

Work at Kester Solder in Chicago proved to be one of my toughest jobs while putting myself through seminary. I transported heavy metals for production of high-quality solder used in circuit boards. A team of nearly fifty people worked with expensive elements like lead, silver, magnesium, titanium, and even gold. Herman Mueller handled all the raw materials with genuine expertise. He did the tough, hot, and dangerous work of mixing molten metals in two-hundred-gallon vats prone to chemical explosions. Herman's arms and face were marked from small burns, his face was always grimy and sweaty, and he only took the shortest of vacations—no sick days.

Herman worked at the very center of the Kester forge, surrounded by six other immigrant smelters, producing the finest (and heaviest) metal slugs to be found in Chicago. The work was tough and no doubt wore him down. But Herman worked full eight-hour days, often overtime, and saved enough energy for weekly victories in the Kester Bowling League. Herman liked metals, but he liked people and their families even more. Preparing, operating, and cleaning a dirty metal room was standard procedure for him. Complaining was not. Herman did everything needed to keep the molten lead and zinc flowing—making the best solder in America.

JIM GARRETT–REAL ESTATE BROKER, BASEBALL UMPIRE

For the short time I worked with Jim, he painted a disciplined picture of dedication to his craft. Jim made his real money as a commercial real-estate broker in Chicago's Loop. But every March, he would begin his annual routine of calling balls and strikes at more than three hundred Illinois high-school baseball games. Not really an athlete, Jim looked more like comedian

Drew Carey—sense of humor included. But he charged into umpiring with the abandon of Pete Rose diving for home plate. After his full day of real-estate deals, Jim would race out to a suburban high-school field and start his real adventure—engineering a fair game for competitive teenage athletes. He knew and remembered coaches, players, good calls, and the ones he wanted to have back.

Umpires like Jim will do everything to get to a game fifteen minutes before shouting "Play ball!" That means changing into their gear at gas stations and racing through yellow lights to get the game started. Men in blue have got to be there for baseball to begin. Jim knows that while he does not play or coach, the game cannot take place without him. He is present and works fast, fair, and hard to pull off a great game.

TODAY'S WORKERS: BETSY AND BILL HOPKINS, WORK FOR LIFE

Betsy and Bill Hopkins are in the busy middle of what they see as a good but not-yet-complete life. Bill is fifty-three years old and Betsy fifty-two—they married thirty years ago when they both finished degrees at Michigan State. Betsy and Bill know how to live cheap and how to live well. They have raised five children: Kate (twenty-eight with two kids of her own), Liz (twenty-six and single), Sam (twenty-five with two children), Clay (twenty-two and just married), and William (nineteen, also a Michigan State student). Life has always been busy for the big Hopkins family. Someone is always borrowing money for a used car, checking out a college, dating a friend's former boyfriend, or shifting career plans on the fly.

As a young man, Bill moved quickly from college to Presbyterian Seminary in Pittsburgh, a few years in the pastorate, and then on to church and nonprofit administration. While a clergyman and administrator, Bill has always been a fundraiser—for churches, mission agencies, colleges, and seminaries. Now, at the apex of his career, he has switched sides and become executive director for Mid-America Mission Fund—one of the largest grant-making foundations in North America. Bill is experienced and savvy and still short of having all the cash he needs to meet Mid-America's wishes.

Personally, Bill is working harder and longer and producing more than he has since his days in seminary. Betsy has relied on all her energy to build a long career in nursing at Carnegie Mellon Health Systems in Pittsburgh. Between babies and church responsibilities, she went on to her master's and has served as a nurse practitioner for the past twelve years. Her income has risen and now rivals her husband's in his new position. Finally, Betsy and Bill are positioned to assist each of their children with education and housing needs. The long career struggle is paying off.

The temptation for Betsy and Bill is to feel they have achieved their goals and then plateau for the next two decades. But as they look at increasing needs in their own extended family (and families around them), the Hopkins's are reevaluating their goals and mission.

Betsy and Bill know that God has blessed them with their will to work and rewarded them richly. They have some things to teach their grandchildren and an extended network of medical and theological students—saints, seekers, and agnostics alike. Bill and Betty want to produce a set of goals focusing on work, production, generosity, and celebration. But they are just beginning that phase of their lives. What is it going to cost them? How much time will it take? Should it be a family project involving all five children, maybe even grandchildren?

Bill and Betty want to produce a set of goals focusing on work, production, generosity, and celebration. But they are just beginning that phase of their lives. What is it going to cost them? How much time will it take?

While these are scary and exciting considerations, Betsy and Bill know that simply living out their years like any other family would be an incomplete decision. They must work with all that God has given them to continue a movement for work and production. Here's what they are thinking so far:

1. God created all people with the capacity to work and produce.
2. Work is hard and often inconvenient, but it is also productive, fulfilling, and financially rewarding. Work is one important way in which we worship God.
3. Work does not come naturally—at least not in twenty-first-century America. People must be taught to work and nurtured in a culture of work, surrounded by achievers among their friends and role models.
4. Work in the decades ahead faces several formidable challenges: technology, leisure, narcissism, and capitalism itself. How do we create a healthy culture of work amid these forces, and how do we add joy to the entire work equation?

Upon their thirtieth wedding anniversary, Bill and Betsy are gathering a group of friends, relatives, and colleagues together with an expert on specific-focus foundations. They want to provide structure for their work legacy, but they are wary of getting too organized. Next month's Work Legacy Planning Retreat at an Allegheny Mountain resort will be a delightful time to gather the people who have known Bill and Betsy for a lifetime. All the kids will be there. They will draw on the memories of what has and has not worked, what is sacred, and what no one has yet thought about. It will be a challenging time that they dare not waste.

CHAPTER 12

SUCCEED AND PROSPER

YOUR WORK RESULTS in more than long hours at the office, loads of meetings, and all your production. In developing effective habits, your work should earn you the money you need to support your family and achieve your financial goals.

The goal of any individual or corporation must be growth and success in the short run so that opportunities for long-term prosperity and success can exist.

As you build your career, begin thinking of your work from a corporate standpoint. Each year's W-2 filing is a state-of-your-personal-corporation annual report. We measure our lives by our family, our loves, the meaning we achieve, the people we help, and the values we develop. Should we not also measure our lives by the most readily available of all stats—our income?

Isn't that too crass? Why be so materialistic? These are fair questions to ask. But how we work, what we achieve, and how much we earn for the important work we do are valid and true measures of our life and the contributions we make to the world around us.

For generations, people have been conscious of their income and wealth. We know what it is to be greedy, selfish, and unconcerned about the needs of people around us. Yet generations of profit-makers have also taught us that work and steady income growth is an important measure of how well we are doing in life. If we apply ourselves to our work in a serious way, chances are that we will be able to increase our income and be able to teach other people how we have driven those year-to-year increases. With annual growth in personal (family) income, we can pay our bills, save for the future, invest in long-term projects, aid the poor, and invest in God's mission.

> ***Yet generations of profit-makers have also taught us that work and steady income growth is an important measure of how well we are doing in life.***

We should be able to reflect on what makes us financially successful, why we are good at the work we do, how we can become better at our work, and how we can teach others the essentials of our success. In turn, we clear the way for the success of many other people.

Think back on your life. The chances are good that you have had a conversation with someone who has taught you the keys to unlock your talents and excel where you have invested yourself. I think of the writers who have told me personal stories on the power of rewriting and editing. I think of the preachers who have gone beyond the details of sermon preparation to teach me about tone, trajectory, and timing necessary for sermons to fire on all cylinders. I think about gardeners and farmers who have shown me good soil and methods to make it better.

These are the people who give us much. Now we must replicate their style and substance in the lives of future workers. We do not give people a free success ticket. Rather, we help young people dig and discover what is already inside themselves. That is how it always happens. Someone helps us find our voice, aptitude, and skills that display all God has built into us.

As a researcher and organizer, I learned many of my own skills through planning an urban consultation for my mentor, Dr. Ray Bakke, and twenty-five of his students in New York City. While the event took only three days, my work covered a period of at least six months. I uncovered the best churches and community organizations in all five New York boroughs for us to visit. I found the most cooperative and knowledgeable people right in their neighborhood contexts. By trial and error, I found the best ways of connecting and transporting my professor and his students through New York's instructive communities.

I relied on new mentors and city experts by listening intently, asking dumb questions, and filling my knowledge base through strategic calls and research. I became a short-term expert on New York City to help build a graduate-level course that changed the lives of many students.

I began by being overwhelmed by the task and realized the best thing I could do was to become a local urban authority. I read, I visited, and I called—all before online communication. I became a 1995 encyclopedia of New York churches, communities, schools, and culture. I worked and the New York City project worked!

Once you have succeeded (once you have become the expert), make it a point to let other people in on your own expertise. There is no hiding your secrets anyway. In the words of Pittsburgh community developer Reid Carpenter, "If it is good, give it away!" People already know why you are good at what you are doing. So, let them in on the full story. The credit often comes right back to you. And if it does not return your way, it multiplies in far more productive directions. Either way you account for it, you are the genius! And you will be delighted by the end results.

Once you have succeeded (once you have become the expert), make it a point to let other people in on your own expertise.

Focus on prospering at what you do. Once you have established a pattern of financial growth, become good at prospering! Enjoy your work, and enjoy the success you have at doing what you do best. Enjoy the details, the problems, the little achievements, and all that goes into making you a good investor, broadcaster, advertising agent, carpenter, diplomat, auto mechanic, or community organizer.

Share with others out of your prosperity, not just your bottom line. The truth is that if you only think of your profit margin, you will not have much to share with anybody. But if you dream, and live out of the prosperity of your work, you will have much to share. Even in lean years, your lessons will virtually teach themselves through your integrity and maturity.

CHAPTER 13

MENTOR OTHERS

MENTORING YOUNG PEOPLE to take up the work you are good at is an admirable task. But why should any of us do that? What does it do for us when we train, encourage, and pave the way for young people to take up our own work and make something greater from it?

Stand back for a moment and review who you are, how you have worked, and what you have contributed to your field. Perhaps you have given a stellar effort and you are proud of what you have done. It may be that you are leaving a legacy with your career, but leaving it to whom?

I am frequently astonished at the sons and daughters of achievers and how they often pick up the skills and habits needed to replace their parents in professional roles. Southern Baptist preacher Andy Stanley is a good example of someone who early on learned by watching his father, Rev. Charles Stanley, love Christ's church and wrestle with God's word. Preaching and leading churches became second nature to Andy Stanley, and it is no wonder that his work has outpaced his father's substantial preaching, teaching, and writing ministries.

Dr. Rand Paul is a US senator from Kentucky. Like his father, Dr. Ron Paul, he made a midcareer transition from medicine to public policy and elective office. The senior Paul is an independent Republican with a Libertarian bent, as is his son Rand. Both doctor/politicians have championed nontraditional third-party causes, displaying a strong backbone in the face of political opposition. Both have campaigned for president of the United States—the father in 1988 and the son in 2016. As a young man, Rand worked on his father's house and presidential campaigns, acquiring much of the senior Paul's thoughtful, inventive spirit. As a senator, Rand Paul has emerged from his father's shadow to become the nation's premier voice on constitutional conservatism. Dad's tenacity and mild crankiness have matured in Rand through his term as Kentucky senator. Political ambition is as natural as growing corn or preaching sermons. These guys have been naturally mentored by their fathers to become an even better version of dad.

Imagine a bright, hardworking college graduate who has only a foggy idea of where his career should take him. You look at this young man, and you see a version of yourself at his own age—all the tools, all the people skills, just lacking direction, connections, and some smoother edges. You are the veteran worker who can help make him a success. You are a mentor.

Are we to replicate ourselves in the lives of young people? Hardly! That would be asking a wrong question. Everyone is equipped to carve out their own future. But every young person needs and deserves the help that a veteran can bring to the task of beginning, honing one's skills, and succeeding in a big way. So many young people have not had natural mentors. The need for intentional mentors has never been greater.

Our work society stands at the crossroads of expanded, elevated expectations and diminished family connections to help make real careers happen. Far too many young people are burdened by student debts that frustrate their beginning careers. We have never had so great a societal need for mentors to get into action in creating a way forward for the young and eager.

Everyone is equipped to carve out their own future. But every young person needs and deserves the help that a veteran can bring to the task of beginning, honing one's skills, and succeeding in a big way.

As a mentor, you get the satisfaction of seeing the best of yourself transplanted into lives of great potential. You also gain the gift of meaningful connections to a new generation of workers who will do things well and do things differently. As mentors, you will become senior learners of the tasks, skills, and habits most needed for the future. While I will only be around for a couple of decades at most, I am excited by the chances to glimpse into the future and to enjoy what I see. It is as if my own work has paved the foundation for a future that belongs to young people.

CHAPTER 14

WHY WE NEED MORE WORKERS

Work is the solution to many personal and systemic issues facing twenty-first-century Americans. Specifically, we need to work more and we need to work harder. We need to make more money and save more money. We need to challenge ourselves to try harder at our present work, and we need to seek out new work because nothing lasts forever.

American's need to create a new culture of work by

- teaching productive skills to young people: from middle school right up through college;
- assigning real household jobs to all family members—young is the time to start working;
- working more hours and rewarding employees for their achievements;
- creating incentives for greater productivity at every kind of job;

- measuring individual production (both quantity and quality) and heightening those production levels with bonuses for exceeding goals;
- dreaming and imagining production levels we have not thought possible. We can do the unimaginable and in turn grow as achievers.

Work is also the problem and the crisis undermining our twenty-first-century society. We are living off the fun and labor-saving functions of a technology revolution that began with video games of the 1980s and grew to occupy all aspects of our waking hours with Facebook, Twitter, YouTube and Instagram. We now do our banking, talking, celebrating, and praying online. It has made for less-fulfilling work and less-satisfying recreation than our predecessors enjoyed in previous eras. How can we play and celebrate without knowing the exhaustion of an achievement-filled workday? Easy has become too simple—no challenge, no achievement, no growth, and no satisfaction.

In a recent study of twenty- to thirty-year-olds in Chicago, researchers found unemployed men spending between thirty and thirty-five hours each week playing video games. Those hours and effort are the equivalent of what many people call a full-time job. But nobody is earning a salary for winning the *Full Metal Jacket* marathon tournament. Nobody is paying rent and utility bills by whiling away another thirty hours on *SimCity*. Life is now play, work is demeaned, and money is not respected.

My home, Chicago, has long been known as the city that works. But no longer do we really work. We no longer have big shoulders, expansive will, nor the enlarged character needed to hold down jobs that support an entire family. We say we want to work as groups and be part of a team. But the truth is that we look for individual assignments allowing us to work singly from home. We are left with little accountability, decreased production, and less money for our efforts.

Where do we gain the instinct to work? Play may be built into human DNA, but the instinct to work (both will and skills) comes through parental modeling and practiced disciplines carried out over long periods of time. Work is not all fun. It is often hard and demanding, inconvenient and tiring. Frequently, work is not even fair. Sometimes we are not appreciated by our bosses, and we come away from doing good work not even appreciating ourselves. Still, meaningful work goes on.

We have a need for the money we earn from our production. We also have the need for meaning that jobs provide. The schedule, the challenges, and the people we work with combine to form the fabric of our work experience. Our world has an insatiable need for what we produce: meals, reservations, metals, novels, medical records, interest rates, smartphones, or civil laws. Put simply, the world needs our stuff. Add to all that the fact that God assigns us work. He calls us to be stewards over all that he first created. Sounds like a higher calling than simply going to work. Our human efforts really do count.

If our future depends upon our work, we had better become good at our work and carrying out our vocations. We need more people who are habitually productive and naturally excel at their work. We also need people who are good at teaching and modeling their work for others to learn from. Further, we need people who are effective at coaching new workers and creating jobs where work seems to be unavailable. Increasingly, work does not seem to be available for people who need to work most.

Put simply, the world needs our stuff. Add to all that the fact that God assigns us work. He calls us to be stewards over all that he first created.

Late twentieth-century emphases on community and persons have not served us well in terms of work needing to get done in this present century. Community developers and activists have campaigned for corporations to locate workplaces where underemployed people already live. That dynamic (or expectation) does not work and never has worked. Work has always moved to locations abundant in business resources: fertile land, low taxes and tariffs, available transportation, and few government restrictions. People have always followed work, moving to the American colonies, Australia, Detroit, the Dakota oil fields, or the Silicon Valley.

Profit-making corporations have always needed substantial workforces to thrive and profit. But corporations will always make decisions on production, location, and salary based on their own needs. They are selfish, and they must be to fulfill their profit-making mission. Individuals and families must follow work in moving to inconvenient locations and unknown ways of life—right along with the corporations that are willing to employ them. This is a healthy reality for work.

You Need to Work:
I write and publish these stories about work and workers because you and I need to work. We need to provide money for ourselves, our families, sometimes our friends, and even for strangers. The personal need for money (and then a good bit of savings) is a growing concern for people worldwide. We cannot look to governments, churches, or charitable institutions to meet our needs for food, housing, transportation, health, and communication. Financial resources for purchasing these goods and services will be earned by the work of individuals and families. And that work is what we can get excited about. Work produces worthwhile rewards in the form of monetary income. And a growing income is a basic human right that we should each desire. We

need to regularly grow our expectations for good rewards from our labor.

We Need More Workers:
Yes, we do need more workers—not just trained workers but employed and wage-earning workers. A latent (yet prevalent) attitude says that most of the important discoveries have been made and nearly all the world's infrastructure has already been built. For the generations ahead, our task is to manage that ever-growing package of wealth, grow our technology, and hold in check our appetite for using natural resources. Such a low-level world view will leave us poor and dying.

Our world needs achievers who throw themselves into their work, produce increasing numbers of products, and reach goals that past generations have either failed to achieve or even recognized as valuable standards. We must enlist ourselves in a movement as producers of material wealth and stewards of the achievement spirit. We must dedicate ourselves to better production and greater standards of service to our families by anchoring ourselves to the creative and saving God. As we focus on work, growth, and production, an inevitable optimism and curiosity will arise within us. We will be excited about the future of work because we will realize all there is yet to be discovered and produced.

In work, we find the meaning of our lives. We have recently thought that life is made of the experiences we collect and the number of interesting human relationships around us. These experiences may be rewarding, but they are not the point of life. We have each been called to work and production as well as love and obedience to our Creator and Savior. As we invest ourselves in the work given us to complete, we find the real purpose of our lives. Our work is not the means to a good end. Our work is God's ordained end for each of us.

God created us to produce, serve, and profit in our efforts. Such production and profit are signs that we believe in the future—the new heaven and new earth that God is creating and of which our salvation is a part. As we work, God smiles upon our efforts and the results we produce. He enjoys the productive efforts and genius we display. He created us for work and production. And we praise his name as we serve him.